Personnel Training Manual for the Hospitality Industry

Copyright © 1991 by Van Nostrand Reinhold

Library of Congress Catalog Card Number 90-24736
ISBN 0-442-23534-8

All rights reserved. No part of this work covered by the copyright hereon may be reproduced or used in any form or by any means—graphic, electronic, or mechanical, including photocopying, recording, taping, or information storage and retrieval systems—without written permission of the publisher.

Manufactured in the United States of America

Published by Van Nostrand Reinhold
115 Fifth Avenue
New York, New York 10003

Chapman and Hall
2-6 Boundary Row
London, SE 1 8HN

Thomas Nelson Australia
102 Dodds Street
South Melbourne 3205
Victoria, Australia

Nelson Canada
1120 Birchmount Road
Scarborough, Ontario M1K 5G4, Canada

16 15 14 13 12 11 10 9 8 7 6 5 4 3 2 1

Library of Congress Cataloging-in-Publication Data

Miller, Jack E., 1930–
   Personnel training manual for the hospitality industry / Jack E. Miller, Mary Walk.
     p.   cm.
   Includes index.
   ISBN 0-442-23534-8
   1. Food service employees—Training of—Handbooks, manuals, etc.u.
I. Walk, Mary.   II. Title.
TX911.3.T73M55   1991
   647.95'068'3—dc20   90-24736

*To: Chester
   and a miracle*

Contents

Chapter 1—Training and Employee Need	**1-1**
Introduction	1-1
Labor Trends	1-2
Chapter 2—Recruiting and Selection	**2-1**
Recruiting	2-1
Selection	2-5
Legal Aspects	2-10
Forms	2-17
Chapter 3—Job Standards	**3-1**
Performance Standards	3-4
Job Breakdown	3-5
Job Descriptions	3-5
Job Specifications	3-6
Forms	3-8
Chapter 4—Company Standards	**4-1**
Employee Handbook	4-2
Policy and Procedures Manual	4-13
Safety Checklists	4-22
Developing Wage Plan Policy	4-29
Sanitation Forms	4-36
Wage Policy Worksheets	4-75
Chapter 5—Training Employees	**5-1**
Orientation	5-1
Checklist	5-2
Job Training	5-3
Cooperative or Apprentice	5-8

Principles for the Trainee	5-10
Instructor Principles	5-11
Forms	5-15

Chapter 6—Training Fundamentals — 6-1
Character of Employees	6-1
The Adult Learning Process	6-2
Job Instruction Training	6-3
A Training Plan	6-4
Training Problems and Training Benefits	6-6
Forms	6-9

Chapter 7—Training Systems and Aids — 7-1
Methods of Training	7-1
Developing a System	7-6
Implementation and Maintenance of a Training System	7-10
Training Room Checklist	7-11
Forms	7-17

Chapter 8—Labor Control — 8-1
Labor Cost	8-1
Estimating Labor Into the Budget	8-2
Calculation of Labor Costs	8-3
Establishing Realistic Standards	8-5
Scheduling for Productivity	8-8
Personnel Requirement Guide	8-10
Physical Factors	8-11
Sales Monitoring	8-14
Improvement Procedures	8-16
Forms	8-20

Chapter 9—Training Evaluation — 9-1
Evaluation Factors	9-1
Employee Tenure Checklist	9-3
Performance Appraisal Program	9-5
Forms	9-9

Appendix A
State Supervisory Personnel for Marketing Education	A-1
Publications	A-8
Videos	A-9

Appendix B
Apprenticeship Programs	B-1
Accreditation Activity	B-9

Acknowledgments

A book of this nature is the result of many years of gathering and collecting. Over the years, we have saved articles, workbooks, seminar handouts, and books; everything that relates to employee training. We are grateful to all the people who write or speak in the complex field of training personnel for food service operations. Dr. Lewis Forrest, for example, is recognized as a leader in providing usable materials for employee training. We are particularly grateful for the insight he provides about workable methods of training employees.

This book has been influenced by the writings of Robert J. Martin in his book, *Professional Management of Housekeeping Operations*. He provides readers with excellent explanations of theory and many practical applications for the supervision of employees.

At the end of each chapter, there is a page of references. If you wish to read further about the material covered in the chapter, these references will provide further insight into the topic. We wish to acknowledge all the people listed in these reference pages. They all contributed to our understanding of the area of food service employee training.

We wish to thank the National Restaurant Association for sponsoring so many opportunities for food service professionals to improve skills and knowledge with seminars, shows, and educational programs. The Educational Foundation of the National Restaurant Association provides many excellent learning experiences for all facets of the food service industry. We have frequently used its educational materials. We particularly want to thank Jeffery Harrison and Jeff Prince for their willingness to share materials with our readers.

We are most familiar with our own state's restaurant group, and we wish to acknowledge the Missouri Restaurant Association and its capable director Carl Degan. He has provided us with concise explanations of current laws affecting those in the food service industry.

One of our staff members, Ted Fournier, introduced the Gantt Chart to our meal planning class. We want to thank him for showing us the practical application of this management device. It helps reduce the anxiety level of our student managers.

A special thanks to a very patient computer whiz, Kay McGee. She is responsible for manipulating WordPerfect and Microsoft Word to create all those good-looking guides, charts, lists, forms and checklists. We would be remiss if we did not also thank our secretary, Pat Kramper, who kept us on track, listened to our frustrations, and translated our words into readable text.

Personnel Training Manual for the Hospitality Industry

Chapter 1

Training and Employee Need

INTRODUCTION

This past year, I decided a bible study class would be good for me. One of the passages we were assigned to read and study spoke about the disciples plucking the ears of grain on the Sabbath. My thoughts wandered back to my younger years and those Sundays I worked brunch in the graduate residence hall. My memories are not walking through wheat fields plucking grain, but plucking juice from the storeroom, cracking eggs, thawing frozen sausage, running clean plates to the serving line, and joking with grousing students. My most vivid memories revolve around the dish machine that should have been replaced a year earlier. Forks were forever getting stuck in the links, the overflow pipe would clog up, and water would spew all over the dishroom. The machine had to be coaxed to run and did not seem to want to work on Sunday, just like the dish crew. We were never told in school what it was like to work on a busy Sunday. It felt like we had to work miracles, feeding hordes of people with just a few loaves and bits of this and that.

This book is about the reluctant dish crew and all the other people working in this labor-intensive hospitality industry. One of the hard lessons for a restaurateur to learn is that the people hired to work in an establishment really do not want to work in a restaurant. If choices were available to the staff of a restaurant, if they could work at any place they wanted, 80 percent would work elsewhere. In fact, if the opportunity arises, 80 percent of the restaurant work force will change jobs.

The people hired often come to us because they have few alternatives. This may be their first job or they have few skills. This may be their first job in this country and the inability to speak the language is a barrier to other opportunities. They really want to have a career elsewhere but are still in school or they cannot find a suitable position. Their first priority is raising a family but we will give them the hours of work that do not conflict with family responsibilities. They already have one job but need another to earn more money. They work in restaurants because jobs are available and they need to work.

LABOR TRENDS

Several factors are compounding the problem of finding suitable employees for restaurant work. The wise operator will understand these factors do exist and will plan strategies to counteract their impact on the restaurant. As the economy changes from a manufacturing- and heavy-industry-based economy to an information- and service-based, economy more companies are looking for the same type of employee. All retailing and banking industry operations are in competition with the hospitality industry for potential employees. The food service industry is growing and competition for employees as well as market share is becoming more intense. Over the years, there has been a major shift in the attitude and values of workers in the United States. Workers expectations have risen. In addition to increased competition and increased expectations, demographic reports (like table 1.1 below) show that a major source of employees for the food service industry, teenagers, is shrinking.

Demographic studies indicate a significantly different work force composition by the year 2000. The labor force from which restaurateurs draw employees will be somewhat older, the share of

Table 1.1 Year 2000 Projected Work Force

Age	Work Force	Number
16-19		8,890,000
20-24	16%	13,751,000
25-34	23%	31,657,000
35-44		38,571,000
45-54	50%	30,552,000
55-64	11%	12,970,000
65+		2,394,000

Adapted from: Bureau of Labor Statistics

women will increase, as will shares of blacks, Hispanics, and Asians. The growth of the work force will be the slowest since the 1930s. This slow growth rate tends to slow down economic expansion and the creation of new jobs. The growth will be in the age group 35 to 54. All other age groups are showing a decline in participation in the work force.

The Implications

The results of demographic studies have implications for the hospitality industry and the individual restaurateur. Managing diversity, understanding culturally different workers, and being able to establish good communications with all employees will be key ingredients for the successful restaurateur.

With a labor force that is not showing growth, it becomes important to increase the productivity of those that are working. One trend that is already influencing employee needs is the increase in takeout and delivery, which requires fewer employees to serve the people eating in the restaurant. All studies indicate productivity is going to be a key issue in the success of the growing food service industry.

Higher employee expectations will create a need to address the core issues that relieve employee discontent. The work issues that are controlled by the employer and that produce employee satisfaction and high morale are the following: the opportunity for growth and personal development, good upward communications, and the perception every employee is treated fairly without favoritism.

A Training Book to Solve Labor Problems

All of these trends—growth in the industry, rising expectations, changing labor pool, and the need for increased productivity—indicate an urgent need for increased training and employee development. Corporations and chains have long been active in setting up training systems for new employees. The hospitality industry provides an opportunity for the independent operator to be a successful business person. While this independent operator is able to know employees, treat them as individuals, and provide good upward communication, turnover and the shrinking labor pool will still create problems. It is possible to take a couple of pages from corporate S.O.P. manuals, mix them with the creativity of the entrepreneur, and produce a workable training system. The rewards of such a product are more career employees, a spirit of teamwork within the operation, less turnover, and realistically knowing what to expect of all workers.

The purpose of this book is to introduce you to the tools of labor management and training systems so you can pick the ingredients of a human resource program that best fit your operation. It is our experience that the right form can be a good tool for organizing the workplace. We have included numerous forms that are designed to be put to use in your business. The forms have been placed at the end of each chapter so they may easily be removed. Use the forms as they are or adapt them for your operation and keep the text as a reference manual. Time is always a scarce resource for an individual entrepreneur and the temptation to skip training for the new employee or the stale long-time employee is very great. What this book does is introduce you to some of the best training methods currently available. Take what works for you and try to implement a long-term solution for the difficult problem of employee satisfaction and morale. Your operation will benefit, your customers will benefit, your employees will benefit and, best of all, your profits will benefit.

REFERENCES

Cooper, M. R. and B. S. Morgan, P. M. Foley, and L. B. Kaplan. 1979. "Changing Employee Values: Deepening Discontent?" *Harvard Business Review*, January-February, pp. 117-125.

Foodservice Industry 2000, National Restaurant Association Current Issues Report, 1988, Washington, D.C.

Chapter 2

Recruiting and Selection

For years, the food service industry operated with the belief there would be an almost continuous supply of new employees. Many times the jobs were designed as low skill, entry level positions that would be simple to learn and perform with a minimum amount of training. Our experience with this type work tells us this will soon become boring and workers will want to move on to something else; thus, the position turns over. The job itself builds a continuing circle that causes the problem to repeat. Turnover has been a part of doing business and has worked as long as replacement employees were available.

Without a continuous supply of new employees, we have to take a hard look at how we handle our human resources. The first ingredient of a human resources program is finding new employees. Two factors are involved in the process of finding new employees. The first factor of this personnel function is recruiting and the second is selection. In this chapter of the book, we will look at these two factors and provide you with suggestions, guidelines, and worksheets for successful recruiting and selection. Recruiting should be competitive, aggressive, and continuous. Selection should be appropriate, cautious, logical, and legal.

RECRUITING

With the shift in the growth pattern of the labor force, recruiting becomes an even more important part of labor management for the restaurateur. Think of recruiting as a form of marketing. You are trying to sell jobs to people who might want them. Just as you create an image for the type of food service operation you want to be, you must create an image that your business is a good place to work. You want to have the reputation you are a fair employer who is concerned about the people working in the restaurant.

The main purpose of an aggressive recruiting program is to find the right people to fill your jobs. This will require using a variety of sources for finding employees, making the effort to find good workers a continuous one, and having a competitive approach in searching for employees. Using a variety of methods to attract people to the jobs you have will ensure better results. It is not a good idea to rely on a single source for employees as this makes you vulnerable to change. You are more likely to get the type of people you are looking for through a systematic marketing plan designed to reach your target groups.

Sources for Employees

As an aid to help you find the best sources for employees in your own community, we have created a worksheet titled "Appropriate Places for Recruiting" (Form 2.1). This worksheet contains a list of places that are possible sources of employees. You will need to provide the telephone number. The blank lines at the bottom are for you to add any places that are pertinent to your community. You will notice the columns on the right side of the page titled winner and loser. Over a period of time, evaluate the success or the lack of success of each recruiting source. Evaluate how much time you spend with each source and how many trainable employees you actually hire from each source. Keep score on how you are doing with your recruiting.

The first place you want to look for new employees is your present employees. Your present employees are the ones who know your reputation and understand your standards. Upgrading an employee is good for the morale of all employees. Friends and relatives of current employees can be a good source if you retain control of the process.

With a high school, look for a program that has a work-study component. The coordinator of a cooperative education program or a marketing management program is a good contact for placement of high school students. Other contacts would be guidance counselors or principals. On the college level, check for a hotel/restaurant program or a culinary arts program. The college placement office always posts a list of jobs available for students. There are several places students will go to read bulletin boards when they are looking for jobs—the placement office, financial aid office, Hospitality Studies department office, student union, and even dormitories. Try talking to athletic coaches. Athletes often look for part-time work with flexible hours.

Appendix A contains a list of the people in each state's department of education who administer marketing education. These are the people to contact for a list of schools in your area with a marketing management program. These programs frequently have students who are interested in learning marketing management in a restaurant operation.

State employment agencies can be a resource for employees if they are given good information to screen potential workers. Look for organizations involved with handicapped workers, non-English speaking families, or other special groups that are seeking job placement for their people. Have them look at the workplace and explain the work duties so it is understood what the employee will have to do.

Many states have a program called Support Work that is administered through the Vocational Rehabilitation Office. In this program, job coaches are available to help the disabled person fit into a job situation. A disabled person with the potential ability to perform the work is taken to the workplace by a job coach and is supervised until they are capable of functioning in that position.

Advertising

Advertising in the classified section of the newspaper is a common method of recruiting employees. Run the ads where potential employees will see them. What are the neighborhoods where your employees live? Keep score of the success rate of your classified advertising. What type of ad and what type of newspaper brings the trainable employee to your door? In addition to newspapers, certain radio stations may be a good places to advertise for workers.

Every ad should contain the following information:

◊ What the job is.
◊ What the hours are.
◊ Where you are.
◊ What qualifications are needed.
◊ How to apply—Where, when.
◊ Attractive features of the job.

Spell out all words. Abbreviations look cheap and create the same image (Miller and Porter, 1985). Study other employment ads and make your ad competitive. Extra white space at the top and bottom of the ad sets off the written copy to advantage. An easily recognizable logo will also attract attention. Pay attention to details and get the best possible ad for your money. Remember this is a marketing effort to reach your target of potential workers.

In chapter 3, listing all the positions in an operation is discussed. Keeping track of the positions and the people gives you a way to know your recruiting needs. We believe recruiting is a constant process. There is always a need to find good people who will work for you. Sometimes the need is strong and sometimes the need is light. The worksheet on Form 2.2 helps you keep a running total of how you are doing in the different positions. If you are communicating with your employees you should be able to anticipate fallout. Use this on a regular basis so you may focus recruiting efforts on the positions with the greatest need.

When jobs are plentiful, even your best efforts may give fewer responses than you like or need. If you find that the demographics of a shrinking teenage workforce and an increasing number of food service operations are causing problems, you may need to use a creative problem-solving approach to recruiting. It may be necessary to help potentially good employees overcome personal obstacles to employment.

Recruiting and the Structurally Unemployed

A source of workers that should not be overlooked is the people who are listed as structurally unemployed. These are people who have not been able to overcome obstacles to employment and it will require creative problem solving to bring them within the ranks of the employed. An active recruiting program will aggressively seek the unemployed who are willing and able to be potentially good workers. Even in times of low unemployment, there are sources of workers among the poorest and least educated people within a community. Structural unemployment seems to be growing. There are unemployed who are being left behind walls of frustration by the changing job requirements of service and high-technology industries. The problems that need to be solved can be attacked by answering the following two questions: What are the obstacles that make up the walls that fence these people off from working?; and What can be done to remove these walls of isolation and frustration?

Generally, you will find one or more of these obstacles to employment among the poor and poorly educated: transportation problems, child care problems, language problems, and lifestyle/work skill problems. The creative problem-solving effort should look at the following three areas for possible solutions: community government, company resources, and the people themselves. We have created a worksheet to help you generate creative solutions to these problems (Form 2.3). The left side of the sheet lists the obstacle. Within each section, the following three areas for finding a possible solution are listed: efforts to influence the community, company resources, and helping people help themselves. In each area, we have listed some suggested courses of action. Some of these courses of action have had positive results for other companies. The lower part of each section has blank lines so you may add your own creative solutions.

Any effort to persuade government and community entities to assist in tearing down walls will contribute to a positive public image. Cooperation with other firms to overcome obstacles also contributes to the image that a business is a good place to work. Employees who are able to work because of the active removal of obstacles that fence them into unemployment will provide a reservoir of good will and improve the morale of the workplace.

Remember this is a worksheet, not a specific list of guidelines. You need to work out a program of activity that best fits your time and money resources. Each community has its own way of helping the unemployed and the under-educated. An investigation of your own community will reveal ways to help solve your need for good reliable workers. This is not an easy task and may involve considerable time and effort, but the final result will certainly be worth the time and effort.

SELECTION

Selection should be appropriate, cautious, logical, and legal. The Fair Employment Practices legal requirements state that no person may be denied the opportunity to submit application for employment for a position of his or her choosing. Companies may not discriminate in the hiring of people based on race, color, natural origin, religious preference, age, or handicap. Companies must provide the opportunity for people to submit applications without prejudice. These legal requirements influence every aspect of the selection process. The selection process is the first place where a restaurateur protects against antidiscrimination legal actions.

A well thought-out job specification is the document that guides the selection process. Job specifications are written as job descriptions are prepared. The guidelines for writing job specifications are covered in chapter 3 with a worksheet that helps you put in writing the specific qualifications for each job in your operation. As long as you use the specific qualifications as the decision point for selecting employees, you will have the best protection possible against law suits. You must be able to show that the requirements of the specification are the requirements of the job.

Preliminary Interviews

The first activity in the selection process is a preliminary interview. This is the first contact with an applicant and is an opportunity for good public relations. Remember, you wish to project the image your business is a good place to work. Also remember applicants are potential guests. This preliminary interview is a prescreening process where applicant qualifications are compared with job needs to see if the person has the potential to perform the job.

Some guidelines for conducting this interview are being cordial and helpful, providing privacy for the interview, and telling the person to relax. Try to find out what job the person is seeking and whether that job is available now or will be sometime in the future. Review the work history as stated on the application to determine whether the applicant meets the obvious physical, mental, and skill qualifications. Do not waste time if the applicant is obviously not qualified or if no immediate position is available. Be efficient in informing the applicant about the lack of a position vacancy or a surplus of qualified applicants. All applicants should be told that the hiring decision will be made based on the most qualified person. The preliminary interview sets the stage for the remainder of the hiring process.

The Application Form

Everyone has the right to fill out an application form. Form 2.4 is an example of an application that meets federal requirements for questions to be answered by job applicants. Form 2.5 explains questions that are non-discriminatory and questions that are potentially discriminatory.

The application provides you with important information about each applicant. It tells you how far he lives from the workplace. It gives you an idea of his educational background and job experience. How it is completed tells you if he can write legibly. Always ask the applicant to answer all questions on the form. This tells you how well he follows instructions.

If your job specifications tell you the person must read English, be neat and orderly, and have legible handwriting, the application provides you with this information.

Once the application has been signed, it becomes the property of the applicant and you have no right to change it in any way. Any marks or writing you make on a completed application form will be scrutinized for any indication of discrimination. As you prepare for the interview, make notes on a separate piece of paper, not the application form.

Testing

Tests add objective data to subjective evaluations and are used to provide one more piece of information about the applicant. They can be given before or after the interview and should be relevant to the job. We have listed some of the tests that have been successfully used by companies in the food service industry.

One of the preferred testing publishers is London House in Park Ridge, Illinois. The Personnel Selection Inventory is a test designed by London House for hourly employees. The Personnel Selection Inventory offers a choice of ten test forms that test for one or more of the following: honesty, drug avoidance, nonviolence, employee/customer relations, emotional stability, safety, work value, supervision, validity, employability index, and detailed personal and behavioral history. It is a paper and pencil test that can be administered in less than one hour and costs between $12 and $16. London House states that it meets the current uniform guideline on employee selection procedures regarding the construction, validation, and use of psychological tests.

Another test is the Reid Honest Test by Reid Psychological Systems of Chicago, Illinois. The Reid Honest Test is a four-part pencil and paper test that takes 45 minutes to complete and costs approximately $12. The four parts of the test cover attitude toward punishment for crimes of theft, detailed biographical data, questions about personal honesty, and questions concerning drug use. Reid Psychological Systems state the test has never resulted in a single determination of unfair discrimination in any state or federal jurisdiction.

Another pre-employment test is the TruTest by InterGram Incorporated of Atlanta, Georgia. The test gives scenarios and asks the respondents to give their opinion. The second part of the test is personal information. The cost per test is $15 (Van Dyke and Strick, 1988).

Performance tests written to test for performance standards provide the most reliable information. They provide an objective measure of an applicant's ability to perform on the job and indicate how much further training is needed.

As a condition of employment, you will want the person to meet your local health department's physical examination tests. Your job specifications will have physical requirements for the job, and a physical examination should show if the job candidate meets the requirements.

Interviewing

Interviewing is the most important step in the selection process. In an interview, you separate who will be employed and who will not. An interview also allows you to make the critical assessment of whether the person matches the job and will work productively within your organization. Several guidelines are given for a successful interview process.

Be Prepared.

Look over the application form and prepare questions for anything that is not clear in your mind. Look over the job specification and prepare questions that relate to the needs of the job. Be aware of questions that may be considered discriminatory.

Have a Proper Place.

It is essential for a good interview to have a quiet place free of distractions and interruptions. The first task is to put candidates at ease. If you can make them comfortable and nonthreatened, they are more likely to open up and be themselves (Miller and Porter, 1985).

Get People to Talk.

The best method is to avoid questions that allow candidates to give yes and no answers. It is best to follow a preplanned pattern so you cover the same territory with every applicant. Some suggested questions:

- ◊ Why do you want to work here?
- ◊ What did you like best about your former job? Dislike most?
- ◊ Which past job did you like best? Dislike most?
- ◊ Describe the best boss you ever had.
- ◊ What did you do at your former job?
- ◊ What is your strongest asset?
- ◊ What would you like to know about the job?
- ◊ What would you like to know about the company?
- ◊ What are the most important qualities to be a great waitress (or busperson, cook, pantry worker, dishwasher, and so forth)?
- ◊ Do you have a minimum wage in mind?

Listen.

Listen carefully. You should only talk about 20 percent of the time. You want the applicants to do most of the talking. Applicants usually give you the answers they think you want to hear. So do not hesitate to probe if you are not satisfied or are uneasy about an answer.

Observe.

Look carefully for nonverbal clues that might tell you how applicants feel about this job. See if they feel at ease with people and if they are comfortable talking to people.

Be Realistic.

Tell the applicants about the job. Explain the hours, days of the week, duties, and responsibilities of the job. You want them to really think about whether this is the right job for them. Give applicants an overview of the restaurant and its customers and how the particular job fits into the picture. Applicants will be interested in the pay and opportunities to improve the pay scale. If you think this person is a good candidate, explain the pay and how pay raises are earned.

Evaluate.

Stick closely to the personal qualities and skills needed on the job. Use a rating system matched to the list of specifications for the job; such as (1) exceptional, hire immediately, (2) well qualified, (3) qualified with reservations, and (4) not qualified. Go through the qualifications listed on the job specification and assign a numerical rating. Add the scores to obtain a total. The total score for each applicant can be compared with all the other applicants to see which person has the best score and is the best qualified. As an example, we have rated a mythical person for a hostess job using our sample host/hostess job specifications (Form 2.6).

The Reference Check

Reference checks (in order of usefulness) are as follows:

◊ Personal (face-to-face) meetings are the least available but provide the most accurate information.

◊ Telephone discussions are the next best and most often used approach.
◊ The least desirable reference is the written recommendation, since managers are extremely reluctant to state opinions that may be later used against them in court.

Reference checks allow you to check the accuracy of the data on the application form. Another important question is whether or not references would rehire the person.

The Hiring Decision

After you think about all the information gathered about a job candidate, you make a decision. If a person is hired, she should be notified by phone as quickly as possible. Follow the phone call with a letter that explains the terms of employment and what the next steps are to complete the employment process. If a person is not hired, she should also be notified (usually by mail) that someone with more qualifications was given the job. Thank her for taking the time to apply for the job.

Always try to hire the person who shows the most qualifications. For example, look at the evaluation for the hostess job. The decision on our mythical hostess candidate could only be to train that person to fit the job or not to hire. If she were hired, it would only be with the understanding that she would undergo training for her communication skills and her supervisory/leadership skills.

It is wise to set a probationary period for employment. Make it clear that employment is not considered permanent until the employee successfully completes a period of probation. Even with the most careful and logical selection process, there are things you do not know until the person starts working. If the person is careless about attendance, does not take much interest in learning the right way to do the job, or does not like the customers, do not hope they will change after the period of probation. They will not and you should end employment right away. You could get stuck with an untrainable employee. Check your state regulations on the length of the probationary period.

LEGAL ASPECTS

Discrimination

Since 1963, a variety of federal and state equal employment opportunity laws have been passed. These laws regulate food service employment practices. The Civil Rights Act of 1964, Title VII, prohibits all employer practices that discriminate on the basis of race, color, religion, sex, pregnancy, or national origin (Sherry, 1984).

In recent years, sexual harassment in the workplace has been a major concern. Although this is generally thought of as a women's issue, in an employment context, it applies to both sexes. Sexual harassment is defined to include "any unwelcome sexual advances, requests for sexual favors, and other verbal or physical conduct of a sexual nature when such conduct has the purpose or effect of unreasonably interfering with an individual's performance or creating an intimidating, hostile, or offensive working environment." EEOC guidelines make employers responsible for harassment activities by supervisors, co-workers, and patrons. The offender cannot simply claim no harm was intended. The actions can be punished if they have a harmful effect.

Guidelines specify the steps to prevent sexual harassment in an establishment. Employers must assert that sexual harassment is against the law and will be grounds for termination. Raise the subject of harassment with all employees. Express strong disapproval, develop appropriate penalties, inform employees of the right and how to complain, and develop methods to make everyone fully aware of the problem and prevention.

Employers may also be held liable for sexual taunts, lewd or provocative comments and gestures, and sexually offensive touching by patrons if the employer was told of the harassment and the harassment was related to the employment activities of the victim. As an employer, you will be liable for harassment of your employees by patrons if you knew or should have known of the conduct and failed to stop it (Sherry, 1984).

The Rehabilitation Act of 1973 requires affirmative action in hiring handicapped workers by employers holding federal contracts in excess of $2,500. The food service for an institution that receives federal money would be covered. The Act also covers both physical and mental handicaps. Generally, a person may not be excluded from a position because of a handicap that has no relation to the job. Court cases have ruled that a person with a contagious disease may be considered handicapped under the statute and may have the protection of that law.

The Age Discrimination in Employment Act of 1967 as amended in 1978 and 1986 prohibits employment discrimination against persons above age 40. You may, however, differentiate between younger employees and minors in the type of jobs given (Sherry, 1984).

Enforcement

Federal, state, and local laws may act in concert or independently of each other. Employers may be subject to three separate levels of law regarding employee rights. Under federal law, the EEOC must first permit the state agency to attempt to resolve an employment discrimination. State and local laws may cover other areas not regulated by federal acts.

Although there are some local variations, the enforcement of antidiscrimination laws follows a highly standardized system. First, a complaint is filed with the Equal Employment Opportunity Agency. Then an investigation is conducted and a finding is made. About half the cases are in favor of the charging party and an attempt is made to resolve the case through a negotiation process. Most cases are settled through the negotiations. Legal action is begun only after attempts at negotiation have failed.

If you become involved in an investigation of a discrimination charge, you should understand the information the investigator needs. There are three categories of employment discrimination: Evil Motive, Differential Treatment, and Disparate Impact. The investigation of Evil Motive looks for documented use of slurs (racial, sexual, age, and so forth), evidence employees of the same class as the charging party consistently fared worse than others, testimony of witnesses to apparently racially motivated actions by the accused, and documented history of previous discriminatory behavior by the accused.

The investigation of Differential Treatment looks for answers to the following questions: What happened to the charging party?; What were the circumstances?; What other employees were in similar circumstances?; What happened to these other employees. The record search for this type investigation can be very burdensome and time consuming.

The investigation for Disparate Impact looks for evidence a particular employment mechanism adversely affects a particular group and how, and the validity of the employment criteria. If it is valid from a business standpoint, it is probably legal. If a criteria for employment is not valid from a business standpoint, why have that criteria?

Illegal Alien

Under the Immigration Reform and Control Act of 1986, every employer must verify the employment eligibility of every new person hired since November 6, 1986. The law requires the following five things:

1. Have employees fill out the Employment Eligibility Verification form, Form I-9.

Recruiting and Selection

2-13

2. Check employee documentation of identity and eligibility to work.

3. Complete Form I-9.

4. Keep Form I-9 for three years, or one year after employment ends—whichever is later.

5. Have Form I-9 available for inspection by INS or U.S. Department of Labor officials.

Documentation must be completed within three days of hire in most cases. All job applicants should be asked, "Are you legally authorized to work in the United States?" Documentation is required only after a person is employed. If an employee is hired for less than three days, the employer must fill out Part 2 of Form I-9 by the end of the first day of employment. If a new hire needs more than three days to obtain the documentation, the new hire must give the employer a receipt indicating the needed document is being sought. If the necessary document is not received by the twenty-first day of employment, the new hire should be removed from the payroll.

The employer needs to examine documents that prove that the people hired are who they say they are and that they are authorized to work in the United States. The documents that are acceptable are listed below.

Documents Acceptable for BOTH Identity and Eligibility
◊ United States Passport
◊ Certificate of United States Citizenship (INS Form N-560 or N-561)
◊ Certificate of Naturalization (INS Form N-550 or N-570)
◊ Unexpired Foreign Passport
◊ Alien Registration Receipt Card ("green card"), provided it contains a photograph of the bearer. Both the old alien card (Form 1-151) and the new alien registration card (Form I-551) (which is white) are valid.
◊ Temporary Resident Card (INS Form I-688)
◊ Employment Authorization Card (INS Form I-688A)

Documents for Identity Only
◊ State-issued driver's license or identification card with photograph. If the driver's license or identification card does not contain a photograph, identifying information, such as name, date of birth, sex, height, color of eyes, and address should be included.
◊ School identification card with a photograph.
◊ Voter's registration card.

- ◊ United States Military Card or draft record.
- ◊ Military dependent's identification card.
- ◊ Identification card issued by federal, state, or local government agencies.
- ◊ Native American tribal documents.
- ◊ United States Coast Guard Merchant Marine Card.
- ◊ Driver's license issued by a Canadian government authority.

Documents for Eligibility Only

- ◊ Social Security card, other than its face "not valid for employment purposes."
- ◊ An original certified copy of a birth certificate issued by a state, county, or municipal authority bearing an official seal.
- ◊ Unexpired INS employment authorization.
- ◊ Unexpired re-entry permit (INS Form I-327).
- ◊ Unexpired Refugee Travel Document (INS Form I-571).
- ◊ Certificate of birth issued by the Department of State (FS-545).
- ◊ Certificate of birth abroad issued by the Department of State (DS-1350).
- ◊ United States Citizen Identification Card (INS Form I-197).
- ◊ Native American Tribal Document.
- ◊ Identification Card for Use of Resident Citizen in the United States (INS Form I-179).

Employers may not insist on the employee's submission of particular documents. As long as the documents appear valid, they are acceptable. An employer may use an outside clearinghouse to handle the verification process. However the employer remains responsible for compliance with the law. An employer does not have to verify the legal status of independent contractors. Whether an individual is an independent contractor will be determined on a case-by-case basis.

The record keeping requirements of this law state that an employer must keep the Form I-9 and any supporting documents for three years or for the duration of the employee's employment plus one year. It is not required that this information is kept in the employee's personnel file. The Immigration and Naturalization Service will give three days notice before any inspection of the Form I-9s (Degan, 1987). The burden of proof lies on the employer. It is the employer's responsibility to see that the required documentation and proof of a person's right to work is completed.

Equal Pay Act

The Equal Pay Act of 1963 requires employees of both sexes receive equal pay for equal work. The courts have interpreted the word "equal" to mean substantially equal. The law may not be evaded by simply making minor changes in the work done. The law is administered by the Equal Employment Opportunity Commission and applies when men and women are employed in substantially similar jobs requiring equal skill, effort and responsibility, and is performed under parallel working conditions. An employee who is discriminated against, must be paid the same wage as other employees in similar jobs (Sherry, 1984).

Record Keeping

Any major action taken with employees should be kept in writing. All of the documents used within the hiring process (all payroll records and any major incidents with employees) should all be in writing and kept in the employee's file. This includes promotions, disciplinary actions, terminations, and work evaluations.

It is a good idea to keep a record of every accident involving employees. In case of death or injury to five or more people, an accident report must be filed with the Department of Labor.

Accurate, up-to-date wage and tax records are an essential management responsibility for all employers. The government is presumed right in tax cases, with the burden on the employer to prove otherwise. Records that must be kept for two years are: basic employment and earnings records; order, shipping, and billing records; records of additions to or deductions from wages paid; and explanations of any wage differentials based on sex for employees within the same establishment. Records that must be kept for three years are: payroll records; all collective bargaining agreements, plans, trusts, and employment contracts affecting wages authorized under the FLSA; sales and purchase records; and employee identity and eligibility documentation.

All records must be kept in a secure place on the premises of the establishment. EEOC inspectors, INS officials, and Wage and Hour representatives are entitled to access to these records for inspection and copying (Sherry, 1984).

REFERENCES

Degan, Carl. 1987. "Immigration Reform Enforcement NOW Scheduled to Begin July 1," *MRA Bulletin*, 15 (11): 1-4.

Forrest, Lewis C., Jr. 1990. *Training for the Hospitality Industry*, East Lansing, MI: Educational Institute of the American Hotel and Motel Association, pp. 49-65. Dr. Forrest has a chapter on hiring trainable employees.

Harrison, Jeffery A. 1990. *The Labor Issue: Hiring, Training and Retaining*, Chicago: The Educational Foundation of the National Restaurant Association, p. 34. This is the resource book that is used for the seminar.

Martin, Robert J. 1986. *Professional Management of Housekeeping Operations*, New York: John Wiley and Sons, Inc., pp. 142-156. Robert Martin has a chapter on staffing procedures.

Miller, Jack E. and Mary Porter. 1985. *Supervision in the Hospitality Industry*, New York: John Wiley and Sons, Inc., pp. 111-126. Jack Miller and Mary Porter have a chapter on recruiting and selection.

Mood, Lester E. *Coping With Anti-Discrimination Laws*, publication unknown.

Sherry, John E. H. 1984. *Legal Aspects of Foodservice Management*, New York: John Wiley and Sons, Inc., pp. 84, 85, 87, 94, 118, 119.

Van Dyke, Thomas and Sandra Strick. 1988. "New Concepts to Old Topics: Employee Recruitment, Selection and Retention," *Hospitality Education and Research Journal*, 12 (2): 363 and 365.

Form 2.1

APPROPRIATE PLACES FOR RECRUITING

	Telephone	Winner	Loser
Upgrade a Current Employee			
Friend of Current Employee			
Relative of Current Employee			
Sales Representatives for Suppliers			
Trade Association			
State Employment Agency			
State Vocational Rehabilitation Offices			
High Schools			
Colleges			
Job Fairs			
Community Organizations			
Bulletin Boards			
Personal Contacts			

Form 2.2

RECRUITMENT PLANNING

Function	Par	− On Hand	+ Fallout	Need to = Hire
Host & Hostess				
Cocktail Waitress				
Bartender				
Bus Person				
Wait Staff				
Prep Cook				
Line Cook				
Dishwasher				
Miscellaneous				

Source: Jeffery Harrison, *The Labor Issue: Hiring, Training and Retaining.*

Form 2.3

OBSTACLES TO EMPLOYMENT

TRANSPORTATION	*Efforts to influence the community.* Work with local authorities to modify the public transportation system. Support private transportation operators. *Company resources.* Provide company-owned vehicles and drivers. Share employee transportation system with nearby business operators. *Helping people help themselves.* Assist employees in forming a car pool. Help with financing. Provide bonus for driver of other employees.
CHILD CARE	*Effort to influence the community.* Support government day care center or tax subsidies for single working parents. *Company resources.* Provide company-owned day care center. Share a day care center with a nearby business. *Helping people help themselves.* Assist employees in setting up an informal day care system. Provide flexible hours.

Form 2.3 (continued)

LANGUAGE	*Efforts to influence the community.* Support English remedial or English improvement classes in local school district. Support English as a Second Language courses in local school district. Vote for tax issues supporting adult education. _____ _____ *Company resources.* Use pictures to communicate. Use color codes to mark things. Provide a translated version of procedures. Provide language instruction for supervisors. Teach English as a part of regular training. _____ _____
LIFE-STYLES/ WORK SKILLS	*Efforts to influence the community.* Press for government programs such as Job Corps. Cooperate with grant programs under the Job Partnership Act. _____ _____ *Company resources.* Create special "apprenticeship" programs—some real work, some counseling, some skill training, and so forth. _____ _____ *Helping people help themselves.* Encourage a one-to-one "mentor" program. Have seasoned employees assist culturally impoverished employees. Provide bonus for an employee sponsoring a less able worker. _____ _____

Recruiting and Selection

Form 2.4
PRE-EMPLOYMENT APPLICATION

EMPLOYMENT APPLICATION Date _____

(Please type or print. If you need additional space, please attach a second sheet)

Position applied for:	Salary Expected:	Permanent ___ Fulltime ___ Temporary ___ Parttime ___

Full Name: _____ Last _____ First _____ Middle

Social Security Number: _____

Present Address: _____ Phone #: _____

Permanent Address: _____ Phone #: _____

Have you ever worked under another name? Yes ___ No ___ List: _____

EMPLOYMENT RECORD

List last position first. (Failure to accurately account for all periods during the last seven years may lead to your application not being considered or, if omissions or falsifications are discovered subsequent to your employment, such omissions or falsifications will be sufficient cause for discharge. Periods of School should be listed by listing the School in the name of the Company and listing the dates attended.)

1
Starting Date	Name of Company:	Supervisor's Name:
Leaving Date	Job Titles & Duties:	Company Phone #:
Rate of Pay		Reason for Leaving:

Were you unemployed between positions? Yes ___ No ___ How Long? ___ Why? ___

2
Starting Date	Name of Company:	Supervisor's Name:
Leaving Date	Job Titles & Duties:	Company Phone #:
Rate of Pay		Reason for Leaving:

Were you unemployed between positions? Yes ___ No ___ How Long? ___ Why? ___

3
Starting Date	Name of Company:	Supervisor's Name:
Leaving Date	Job Titles & Duties:	Company Phone #:
Rate of Pay		Reason for Leaving:

Were you unemployed between positions? Yes ___ No ___ How Long? ___ Why? ___

4
Starting Date	Name of Company:	Supervisor's Name:
Leaving Date	Job Titles & Duties:	Company Phone #:
Rate of Pay		Reason for Leaving:

Were you unemployed between positions? Yes ___ No ___ How Long? ___ Why? ___

Have you ever been asked to resign or been fired for cause? Yes ___ No ___

May we contact your previous employers? Yes ___ No ___ . Please list by number the employers you wish us not to contact. _____

If presently employed, why do you desire to change employment? _____

Have you ever worked for this Company before? Yes ___ No ___ When? _____

Reprinted with permission of Missouri Restaurant Association.

Form 2.4 (continued)

EDUCATIONAL RECORD

Number of years completed? 1 2 3 4 5 6 7 8 9 10 11 12 13 14 15 16 17 18

	Name and Location	From 19	To 19	Graduated	Major Course Work
Grammar School					
High School		19	19		
College		19	19		
Other		19	19		
		19	19		

Please list any outside school activities you were active in: _____

GENERAL INFORMATION

Are you older than 18 but less than 70? Yes _____ No _____   Are you older than 21? Yes _____ No _____

Have you any physical defects that would prevent you from performing the duties of the position that you are applying for? Yes _____ No _____ . If "Yes" please list: _____

Have you ever received Workman's Compensation? Yes _____ No _____ If "Yes" explain: _____

Do you have transportation to and from work? Yes _____ No _____

What shift are you willing to work? Day _____ Night _____ Swing _____ Any _____

Will you work: Saturday _____ Sunday _____ Holidays _____

Name of any relative working for this Company and their relationship to you? _____

If an alien, do you have a legal right to be in the U.S.? Yes _____ No _____

If an alien, do you have the right to accept employment in the U.S.? Yes _____ No _____

Have you ever been denied a bond? Yes _____ No _____

Is there any reason why you would now be denied bond? Yes _____ No _____

If this box has been checked please fill out ☐ Uniform size needed _____

List additional names of people working here who know you very well. _____

In case of emergency please notify: _____ Relationship _____

Address _____ Phone #: _____

MILITARY RECORD

Are you now or have you ever been in the military? Yes _____ No _____

If "Yes": Branch of service? _____ From _____ To _____ Honorable Discharge _____

Highest Rank Obtained? _____ If in Reserves: Active _____ Inactive _____

IMPORTANT—PLEASE READ CAREFULLY

I hereby authorize investigation of all statements contained in this application, including inquiry of any and all of my former employers or references as indicated elsewhere in the application and hold said former employers and/or references harmless from liability arising therefrom. I affirm that all the information contained in this application is true and correct and that any misrepresentation, falsification or omission herein shall be sufficient reason for dismissal from, or refusal of employment. If employed, I hereby agree to abide by all policies and rules of this Company which govern dress, hair, grooming and attitude.

Date: _____ Signature _____

Form 2.5

E.E.O.C. GUIDELINES FOR PRE-EMPLOYMENT INQUIRES

> The burden of proof is often on you, the employer, to show that use of information regarding applicants is not discriminatory. Thus, your pre-employment inquiries should be carefully reviewed to assure that their use is job related and not discriminatory. The questions below are examples of acceptable questions as opposed to those of a potentially discriminatory nature. The potentially discriminatory questions are those that tend to disproportionally reject females and/or minorities and are difficult to prove as job related.

NONDISCRIMINATORY INQUIRIES*	POTENTIALLY DISCRIMINATORY
(if used, they should be asked of everyone)	
Race, Religion, National Origin	
	What is your race/religion/national origin?
Arrest and Conviction Records	
Have you ever been convicted of a crime? If so, when, where, and disposition of case?	Do you have an arrest record? (Arrest is not an indication of guilt. Minorities as a group are more likely to have arrest records.)
Family or Marital Status	
Do you have any activities, commitments, or responsibilities that will prevent you from meeting our work attendance requirements? Can you meet our work schedules of _____ ?	What is your marital status? Are you widowed, separated, or divorced? Do you have small children at home, and if so, do you have adequate provisions for child care? (These questions often screen out more women than men. Marital status should not be used to assume greater absenteeism or turnover.)
Financial Situation	
What are you looking for in terms of a a salary? This position pays _____. Is that acceptable?	What charge accounts do you have and how is your credit? Do you own your own home?

Source: Missouri Restaurant Association

* Be certain to check your State Fair Employment Practice laws. Some states explicitly forbid certain questions not specified

Form 2.5 (continued)

NONDISCRIMINATORY INQUIRIES	POTENTIALLY DISCRIMINATORY
	Do You have a bank account? (These questions more often screen out minorities. Previous work history is a more valid measure of job stablility.)
Transportation	
Do you have transportation to work?	Do you own your own car?
Religion	
Are you available for Saturday and/or Sunday work? (If asked, indicate that reasonable efforts will be made to accomodate religious needs. This is required by law unless it creates undue business hardship, which is difficult to prove.)	Do you regularly attend religious services? What is your religious affiliation?
Organizational Membership	
What organizations, clubs, societies, or lodges do you belong to, excluding the names of any that would indicate the race, religion, or national origin of its members?	What organizations, clubs, societies, or lodges do you belong to?
Request for Photograph	
(If necessary, obtaining a photo after applicant is hired is lawful for security or other related purposes.)	Asking for a photograph prior to hiring. (This practice would tend to reveal race, color, national origin, and sex, and therefore could be used in a discriminatory manner.)

Form 2.6

JOB SPECIFICATION

Job Title: Host / Hostess	**Hours of Work:** 5:00 p.m. to 11:00 p.m.

A. Age:
  Must be 21. May be called on to serve alcoholic beverages.

B. Education:
 One year college
 Not always correct English
 Accurate math
  The minimum education requirement is two years of high school. The person must be articulate with grammatically correct English. The person must be able to add, subtract, and multiply accurately.

C. Job Knowledge:
 Two years
  A minimum of six months successful experience as a wait person.

 No supervisory experience
  Six months successful experience in a responsible supervisory job or has demonstrated leadership potential.

 Worked all three positions
  Ability to perform as a wait person, cashier, or bus person.

 Basic understanding
  Basic understanding of food, beverages, service, sanitation, and related equipment and tools.

D. Judgment:
  Must be able to make quick and accurate judgments in the dining area.

E. Physical:
 Apparent good health
  Health, strength, and endurance sufficient to spend 85 percent of time walking and standing without showing fatigue.

 Somewhat casual in dress
  Good posture, graceful carriage, neatness, and good taste in appearance.

 Yes
  Meticulous in personal hygiene.

F. Skill:
 Normal
  Requires a high degree of manual dexterity, precision, and rapid but graceful movements in crowded dining room.

 Normal
  Excellent hearing and vision.

  Sensitivity to the needs of guests.

 Good math, average verbal
  Good verbal and math skills.

Form 2.6 (continued)

G. Characteristics:	
Yes	Requires an outgoing personality.
Maybe	Must be sufficiently aggressive to insist upon meticulous and rigid conformity and standards of service.
Do not know	Must demonstrate leadership ability with other dining room personnel.
Yes	An awareness of the social graces needed for the gracious serving of food and beverages.
Stable	Sufficient emotional stability to handle problems calmly, objectively, and without emotional involvement.
Knows details	Attentive to all the details required for excellent dining room service.
Yes, with reservations	Articulate with an ability to communicate effectively with both customers and staff.

Form 2.7

EMPLOYMENT ELIGIBILITY VERIFICATION

EMPLOYMENT ELIGIBILITY VERIFICATION (Form I-9)

1 EMPLOYEE INFORMATION AND VERIFICATION: (To be completed and signed by employee.)

Name: (Print or Type) Last	First	Middle	Birth Name
Address: Street Name and Number	City	State	ZIP Code
Date of Birth (Month/Day Year)		Social Security Number	

I attest, under penalty of perjury, that I am (check a box):

☐ 1. A citizen or national of the United States.
☐ 2. An alien lawfully admitted for permanent residence (Alien Number A _____).
☐ 3. An alien authorized by the Immigration and Naturalization Service to work in the United States (Alien Number A _____ .
   or Admission Number _____ . expiration of employment authorization, if any _____).

I attest, under penalty of perjury, the documents that I have presented as evidence of identity and employment eligibility are genuine and relate to me. I am aware that federal law provides for imprisonment and/or fine for any false statements or use of false documents in connection with this certificate.

Signature	Date (Month/Day, Year)

PREPARER TRANSLATOR CERTIFICATION (To be completed if prepared by person other than the employee). I attest, under penalty of perjury, that the above was prepared by me at the request of the named individual and is based on all information of which I have any knowledge.

Signature	Name (Print or Type)		
Address (Street Name and Number)	City	State	Zip Code

2 EMPLOYER REVIEW AND VERIFICATION: (To be completed and signed by employer.)

Instructions:
Examine one document from List A and check the appropriate box. **OR** examine one document from List B **and** one from List C and check the appropriate boxes.
Provide the *Document Identification Number* and *Expiration Date* for the document checked.

List A Documents that Establish Identity and Employment Eligibility	List B Documents that Establish Identity	and	List C Documents that Establish Employment Eligibility
☐ 1. United States Passport ☐ 2. Certificate of United States Citizenship ☐ 3. Certificate of Naturalization ☐ 4. Unexpired foreign passport with attached Employment Authorization ☐ 5. Alien Registration Card with photograph	☐ 1. A State-issued driver's license or a State-issued I.D. card with a photograph, or information, including name, sex, date of birth, height, weight, and color of eyes. (Specify State)_____ ☐ 2. U.S. Military Card ☐ 3. Other (Specify document and issuing authority) _____		☐ 1. Original Social Security Number Card (other than a card stating it is not valid for employment) ☐ 2. A birth certificate issued by State, county, or municipal authority bearing a seal or other certification ☐ 3. Unexpired INS Employment Authorization Specify form # _____
Document Identification # _____	*Document Identification* # _____		*Document Identification* # _____
Expiration Date (if any)	*Expiration Date (if any)*		*Expiration Date (if any)*

CERTIFICATION: I attest, under penalty of perjury, that I have examined the documents presented by the above individual, that they appear to be genuine and to relate to the individual named, and that the individual, to the best of my knowledge, is eligible to work in the United States.

Signature	Name (Print or Type)	Title
Employer Name	Address	Date

Form I-9 (05/07/87)
OMB No. 1115-0136

U.S. Department of Justice
Immigration and Naturalization Service

Form 2.7 (continued)

Employment Eligibility Verification

NOTICE: Authority for collecting the information on this form is in Title 8, United States Code, Section 1324A, which requires employers to verify employment eligibility of individuals on a form approved by the Attorney General. This form will be used to verify the individual's eligibility for employment in the United States. Failure to present this form for inspection to officers of the Immigration and Naturalization Service or Department of Labor within the time period specified by regulation, or improper completion or retention of this form, may be a violation of the above law and may result in a civil money penalty.

Section 1. Instructions to Employee/Preparer for completing this form

Instructions for the employee.

All employees, upon being hired, must complete Section 1 of this form. Any person hired after November 6, 1986 must complete this form. (For the purpose of completion of this form the term "hired" applies to those employed, recruited or referred for a fee.)

All employees must print or type their complete name, address, date of birth, and Social Security Number. The block which correctly indicates the employee's immigration status must be checked. If the second block is checked, the employee's Alien Registration Number must be provided. If the third block is checked, the employee's Alien Registration Number *or* Admission Number must be provided, as well as the date of expiration of that status, if it expires.

All employees whose present names differ from birth names, because of marriage or other reasons, must print or type their birth names in the appropriate space of Section 1. Also, employees whose names change after employment verification should report these changes to their employer.

All employees must sign and date the form.

Instructions for the preparer of the form, if not the employee.

If a person assists the employee with completing this form, the preparer must certify the form by signing it and printing or typing his or her complete name and address.

Section 2. Instructions to Employer for completing this form

(For the purpose of completion of this form, the term "employer" applies to employers and those who recruit or refer for a fee.)

Employers must complete this section by examining evidence of identity and employment eligibility, and:
- checking the appropriate box in List A *or* boxes in both Lists B and C;
- recording the document identification number and expiration date (if any);
- recording the type of form if not specifically identified in the list;
- signing the certification section.

NOTE: Employers are responsible for reverifying employment eligibility of employees whose employment eligibility documents carry an expiration date.

Copies of documentation presented by an individual for the purpose of establishing identity and employment eligibility may be copied and retained for the purpose of complying with the requirements of this form and no other purpose. Any copies of documentation made for this purpose should be maintained with this form.

Name changes of employees which occur after preparation of this form should be recorded on the form by lining through the old name, printing the new name and the reason (such as marriage), and dating and initialing the changes. Employers should not attempt to delete or erase the old name in any fashion.

RETENTION OF RECORDS.

The completed form must be retained by the employer for:
- three years after the date of hiring; or
- one year after the date the employment is terminated, whichever is later.

Employers may photocopy or reprint this form as necessary.

U.S. Department of Justice
Immigration and Naturalization Service

OMB #1115-0136
Form I-9 (05 07 87)

Chapter 3

Job Standards

How do you know when someone has done a good job? We know how to judge a good bowl of soup. It has a pleasing aroma, it is the right temperature, it has eye appeal, its serving bowl is attractive, and it tastes good. What do we mean when we say, "Hey Joe! That's a good job"? A performance level, a way to measure quality (good job), a standard that lets everybody know what is expected must be built into a job. If you know how to write recipes that give you good quality food and beverage products, you can write standards for all the parts of a job that will give you good quality performance.

Before beginning, answer the following questions: "Why are standards important?" Why should you spend your time developing job standards? How will job standards help run your business? The purpose of developing job standards is to define a day's work for each job classification and set a standard of performance for that job. This will help you prepare guidelines for hiring the right people to fill your jobs. Job standards will help you develop training plans for each job and written job standards will give you a method of evaluating each employee to see if they are performing a fair day's work.

Now that you know why, begin with the first step. The first step is to develop a list of jobs or job titles that identify each and every position that must be filled. The job title identifies a payroll classification. In order to prepare this list, specify all the tasks in running a restaurant that must be accomplished. Then group these tasks into logical units. Each unit will form a job classification.

In restaurants, this is frequently done by the place where the work is performed. Divide the work into the production or kitchen area and the service or dining area. Then group the tasks according to level of skill. Different skill levels are required as the person gains confidence, knowledge, and speed. There are usually entry level positions in either the kitchen or dining area where a person may grow into a higher level of responsibility. Supervisory skills and task performance skills are separated as these two types of skills are different.

A list of job titles for the dining area may look like this:

- ◊ Host or Hostess
- ◊ Waiter/Waitress
- ◊ Busperson

The number of positions for each job title depends upon the volume of business. It is a good idea to identify each position with a job title and a number. Each position should be based on the job, not the talents of a specific person. When a position opens, it may be identified by its number. When a person is hired, his name may be written into the slot. When volume is low, certain positions may be left unfilled until volume increases (Martin, 1986). Your job list might look like this:

- ◊ Host/Hostess
    1.
    2.
- ◊ Waiter/Waitress
    1.
    2.
    3.
    4.
    5.
    6.
    7.
    8.
- ◊ Busperson
    1.
    2.
    3.
    4.

The job list for the kitchen, of course, depends upon your menu, but it should look something like this:

- ◊ Kitchen Supervisor
    1.
- ◊ Cook
    1.
    2.
    3.

◊ Pantry
  1.
  2.
◊ Pots and Pans
  1.
  2.
◊ Dishwashing
  1.
  2.
  3.
  4.

While the job title identifies a position to be filled, it does not identify the work each person in that position is supposed to do. Clarify in your own mind exactly what you want each person to do. This requires what educators call a job analysis. A job analysis defines what an employee does on the job. It also determines the units of work or sequences of work that are performed for each job. Identify all the units that make up a job classification and the tasks that make up that unit.

We have devised a worksheet (Form 3.1) to assist in analyzing all the jobs in your operation. Since the work of operating a food service falls into some general categories, it is possible to look at these general categories and see which ones apply for a specific job. We have separated the Job Analysis Worksheet into two parts. One part involves technical performance skills and the other part is more involved with knowledge, attitude, or behavior requirements. Use a separate worksheet for each job title listed for your operation. Go through the important work sequences and write down the ones that apply for each specific job. For example, a waitress actually sets up two "work stations." One is the service station in the dining room and the other is the dining table. A waitress may prepare a beverage item and prepare an item for service with the proper plate or garnish. The waitress communicates with the customers, serves food, and handles money.

The list of critical activities should be reviewed and the ones that apply to the specific job under analysis should be written down. These are not work sequences but important activities in the performance of the job. The critical activities will need detailed explanations of a level of knowledge, an attitude, or a type of behavior that is required for the employee. For example, a waitress must have sufficient knowledge of menu items to recognize quality factors. A behavior requirement could state that a waitress should be cordial and pleasant with all customers.

When all the important work sequences and critical activities are listed, list the tasks needed to complete each unit of work. These task sequences answer the question what the employee will do. As an example, the following tasks are part of the communications with a customer:

Unit of Work: Communicate with Customer

- ◊ Greets guests.
- ◊ Explains menu.
- ◊ Takes food and beverage order.
- ◊ Explains wine list.
- ◊ Takes wine order.
- ◊ Checks customer satisfaction.

While job analysis is a time consuming effort, it is the very foundation of the solution to worker performance problems.

PERFORMANCE STANDARDS

This job analysis puts into logical units *all* the tasks that are performed in your restaurant. As an employer, you have the right to receive a fair day's work from each employee. Once you have listed the tasks for each unit of work, you should establish a standard of performance for each unit of work. For example, a food and beverage server takes the food, wine, and beverage orders accurately for a table up to six guests; accurately and legibly completes a guest check; and prices and totals the check with 100 percent accuracy (Miller and Porter, 1985). Measure speed, accuracy, number of units, time, and quality. The performance standard is a crucial step in analyzing the job as it is carried out in your establishment.

The next form (Form 3.2) may be used to write performance standards. Form 3.3 is an example of a completed worksheet. Let us look at a unit of work, "Sets up Work Station," for a server, and the first task, *stocks service station*. Make the description more precise by limiting the scope of the work sequence:

The server will *stock* the service station for one serving area for one meal . . .

Always use an action verb. The use of an action verb and limiting the action makes it easier to observe and measure the performance. State the standard of performance:

. . . completely and correctly in ten minutes or less.

This means that everything must be in its assigned place within ten minutes and nothing must be missing (Miller and Porter, 1985). This is repeated for the second task, *sets or resets a table*.

The last section of this form will help you develop manuals with the specific information needed to complete each task. Most everyone has seen S.O.P.s or standard operating procedures manuals. For example, you may want a checklist of every item needed at the service station. An illustration or a drawing of the layout of the table top may be appropriate. This is the best time for you to write down what is needed. The next step is a job breakdown that will produce the procedure sheets, checklists, illustrations, layouts, and so forth (Forrest, 1990).

JOB BREAKDOWN

When the job analysis was performed, all the tasks needed to perform a unit of work were listed. The job breakdown process refines this list. This process puts into writing the procedures you want your people to follow and gives you a written document that can be used for training each individual to perform the job according to your standards. First, list all the tasks that are performed to complete a unit of work in the order in which they are performed. Then, explain out each task with procedure sheets or layout illustrations that clearly show how you want that task carried out in your operation.

As an example, Form 3.4 is a procedures sheet for "Explains the Menu," which is part of a Wait Person's unit of work, "Communication With a Customer." All of the standard procedure sheets for all the work units and critical activities for a Waiter/Waitress will form a procedures manual for the job of Waiter/Waitress (Forrest, 1990; Miller and Porter, 1985).

JOB DESCRIPTIONS

When you have listed the jobs, determined the units of work for each job, detailed the tasks, and set performance standards, the job descriptions will flow naturally. We have provided a form (Form 3.5) to help consolidate into a working job description all the available information.

A set of job descriptions for all the jobs in your restaurant will ensure that every task is assigned and assignments do not overlap. With sufficient detail, the employee understands what is to be done, how and to what level of performance it is to be done, and what guidelines are available.

A word of caution. Before you begin filling out the form, be careful not to make a job too narrow without even a whisper of risk. Many jobs can be broadened to include responsibility and freedom to make some decisions. Workers respond well to responsibility for their own jobs: they get more done, they become involved in the job, and they take pride in their work.

Consider what the experts say about improving productivity

and job satisfaction for workers. Specific suggestions include making production more personalized and having employees sign their work. For instance, when someone creates a special salad, this can be communicated to the serving person and, in an appropriate manner, to the customer. Positive feedback from the customer relayed by the serving person will give the pantry person a sense of pride and add to a sense of belonging to a team.

Another suggestion is to have subject matter experts. You may find someone in your wait staff has a special flair for serving a flaming dessert. Maybe someone takes a special interest in wine service and can become an expert in suggesting the appropriate wine for each menu item.

In filling out the form, list the duties to be performed in the sequence they are performed. Include the standard of performance required and reference material available that explains the particular task. When all the sequential work has been written, list the critical activities for that job. These critical activities will also have a standard of performance and appropriate reference material. A copy of a completed job description for a Waiter/Waitress (Form 3.6) is included to let you see how a job description will look.

When completing the Job Description, you may want to consider what is the most difficult part of the job or what is most critical to the success of the restaurant. You may wish to give certain items a high priority rating with a suitable reward for excellence.

JOB SPECIFICATIONS

In this chapter, you have been given directions for establishing on-the-job standards of performance. This last section will give you a worksheet for setting a standard in the selection of new employees. A job specification is a listing of skills, abilities, and personal characteristics needed to perform a job. You want to select people that have the potential to do the job with training. In addition to selecting new employees, the job specification provides a standard for upgrading current employees.

Employees should be selected and promoted on the basis of qualifications that match the qualifications needed to perform the job. Written job specifications enable you to do this.

Employers that use written job specifications for hiring and promoting are more apt to comply with anti-discrimination laws. We wrote about the need for restaurants to comply with EEOC laws in Chapter 2. As previously mentioned, any employer may not discriminate in any way on the basis of race, national origin, sex, age, marital or family status, or religion. It is also illegal to discriminate against handicapped persons unless the handicap interferes with the work.

Written qualification standards help you decide who to hire. The job specification takes information provided on other documents and puts it on a form that you can use when you are looking for people to fill a particular job. Using the job analysis and the performance standards for each job, list the physical requirements (for example, meticulous in personal hygiene), the work skills (for example, sensitivity to the needs of guests), mental ability (for example, ability to add, subtract, and multiply accurately), and personal characteristics (for example, an awareness of the social graces) the work requires.

Form 3.7 is a guide for collecting and noting information needed for the job specification. For each job title, look at the list of requirements and note all those that apply. With some, you will want a brief explanation on the extent of the requirement. For example, a host/hostess must have sufficient endurance to spend 85 percent of the time standing and walking without showing fatigue.

When this worksheet is completed (Form 3.8), it provides the necessary information for the job specification. This is an example of a job specification for a hostess. You can see how the worksheet information is put into an easily readable and usable form that would be very helpful in the hiring process. Everything listed on the job specification is essential to the performance of the job.

REFERENCES

Forrest, Lewis C., Jr. 1990. *Training for the Hospitality Industry*, East Lansing, Michigan: Educational Institute of the American Hotel and Motel Association, pp. 30-40, 40-46.

Martin, Robert J. 1986. *Professional Management of Housekeeping Operations*, New York: John Wiley and Sons, Inc., pp. 44, 45.

Miller, Jack E., and Mary Porter. 1985. *Supervision in the Hospitality Industry*, New York: John Wiley and Sons, Inc., pp. 92-97, 153.

Form 3.1

JOB ANALYSIS WORKSHEET

Job Title: _____

Identify important work sequences.

Does the employee:

- Set up a work station?
- Obtain needed materials and supplies?
- Produce food item?
- Produce beverage item?
- Produce clean dishes?
- Produce clean utensils or equipment?
- Communicate with customers?
- Prepare product for service?
- Serve food or beverage item to customer?
- Handle money?
- Provide information for reports?
- Provide input for menu development?
- Participate in promotional activities?

For each sequence of work, list tasks needed to complete the sequence in order performed.

Unit of Work 1.
Task 1.
     2.
     3.
     4.
     5.
     6.

Unit of Work 2.
     1.
     2.
     3.
     4.
     5.
     6.

Unit of Work 3.
     1.
     2.
     3.
     4.
     5.
     6.

Form 3.1 (continued)

Unit of Work 4.
Task 1.
      2.
      3.
      4.
      5.
      6.

Unit of Work 5.
      1.
      2.
      3.
      4.
      5.
      6.

Identify critical activities.

Does the employee:

- Recognize and maintain quality standards?
- Follow sanitary procedures?
- Maintain good customer relations?
- Meet dress and grooming standards?
- Demonstrate creativity?
- Personalize work?

For each critical activity, list the tasks involved or the standard of behavior expected.

Activity 1.
    Tasks
      or
    Behavior

Activity 2.
    Tasks
      or
    Behavior

Activity 3.
    Tasks
      or
    Behavior

Activity 4.
    Tasks
      or
    Behavior

Form 3.2

PERFORMANCE STANDARDS WORKSHEET

Job Title:_____

Unit of Work:_____

What must be done?   *(Describe the performance)*

To what standard: *(A measure of how well the job is done)*

What must be done?   *(A measure of how well the job is done)*

Reference material needed:

   S.O.P.s

   Pictures

   Checklists

   Layouts

   Drawings

   Vidoetape

Job Standards

Form 3.3

PERFORMANCE STANDARDS WORKSHEET

Job Title: _____

Unit of Work: _____*Sets Up Workstation*_____

What must be done?

The worker will stock the service station for one serving area for one meal.

To what standard:

Completely and correctly in ten minutes or less.

What must be done?

Sets or resets a table.

To what standard:

In three minutes or less.

Reference material needed:

S.O.P.—Service Station Procedures

Checklist—Service Station Checklist

Layout—Table Top Layout Sheet

Form 3.4

STANDARD PROCEDURE

Job: Wait Person   **Unit:** Communicate with Customer

Task No. 2: Explain the Menu

1. Customer will indicate verbally or by behavior when they are ready to place the food order. Approach the table at this time.

2. Explain the daily specials and answer any questions about the food the customers have at this time.

3. Ask if the customers are ready to order. Start with the women when writing the orders. Try to stand at each customer's right as you take the order. Children first, women next, and then the men.

4. Help each person plan a complete meal. Be sensitive to what each person wants. Be knowledgeable about the food: where it is from, what is in season, which items complement and enhance each other, and so forth.

5. Answer questions about preparation methods, tastes, and portion sizes.

6. Inform each guest about the approximate cooking times for the selection.

7. Accurately record selection. If you are not clear or if children are being served, repeat selection to the customer.

8. Courteously explain allowable substitutions. If uncertain, ask manager and then go back and explain to the guest.

9. When customers have completed the order, make one last check to see if anything else is needed.

10. Collect the menus and return them to menu holder.

11. Turn in food orders to the kitchen and begin the serving procedure.

Job Standards

Form 3.5

JOB DESCRIPTION

Job Title: _____
Immediate Supervisor: _____
Working Hours: _____
Uniform: _____

DUTIES TO BE PERFORMED	STANDARD OF PERFORMANCE	GUIDELINES AVAILABLE

Form 3.6

JOB DESCRIPTION

Job Title:	_Waiter/Waitress_
Immediate Supervisor:	_Assistant Manager_
Working Hours:	_4:00 p.m. to 10:00 p.m._
Uniform:	

DUTIES TO BE PERFORMED	STANDARD OF PERFORMANCE	GUIDELINES AVAILABLE
Stocks the service station for one meal.	Completely and correctly in ten minutes or less.	Service Station Procedure Sheet
Sets or resets a table.	Properly in three minutes or less.	Table Setting Layout Sheet
Greets guests after they are seated.	Cordially within five minutes.	
Takes the order—Explains the menu to customer.		Menu policy guide
—Describes the day's specials.	Accurately.	Menu posted
—If asked, describes quality or cut, portion size, preparation method.	Accurately.	Recipes Menu meeting
—Specifies items accompanying menu item.		
—If asked, specifies allowable subsitutions	Accurately.	Menu policy guide
—If asked, describes ingredients and taste of any menu item.	Accurately.	
Takes food, wine, and beverage orders for a table.	Accurately and legibly, up to six guests.	Guest Check Procedures Sheet

Job Standards

Form 3.6 (continued)

DUTIES TO BE PERFOMED	STANDARD OF PERFORMANCE	GUIDELINES AVAILABLE
Prices and totals check.	100 percent accuracy.	
Picks up order and completes plate preparation.	Correctly.	Plate Preparation Sheet
Serves a complete meal to all persons at each table in an assigned station using tray service method.	Not more than one hour per table.	Tray Service Sheet
If asked, recommends, opens, and serves wine.	Appropriate to menu item; correctly.	Wine/Food Sheet Wine Service Sheet
Totals and presents check and carries out payment procedures.	100 percent accuracy.	Check Payment Procedure Sheet
Performs side work as assigned.	Correct sanitation level required.	Side Work Procedures Sheet, Sanitation Checklist
Operates all preparation and service equipment in the assigned area.	Correctly, safely.	Operations Procedures Sheet
Meets all the uniform, appearance, and grooming standards.	At all times.	Appearance Grooming Checklist
Observes the sanitation procedures specified for serving personnel and maintains work area.	At all times, 90 percent or higher.	Sanitation Manual, Sanitation Checklist
Maintains good customer relations; maintains a customer complaint ratio.	At all times less than one per 200 guests.	Customer Relations Checklist

Form 3.7

JOB SPECIFICATION

Job Title: _____

Hours of Work: _____

Personal Requirements:

    Age _____

    Appearance _____

    Strength _____

    Endurance _____

    Neatness _____

    Health and Hygiene _____

Posture:

    Standing _____

    Walking _____

    Sitting _____

    Stooping _____

    Reaching _____

    Climbing _____

    Lifting _____

    Other _____

Skills:

    Accuracy _____

    Acuteness of Senses _____

    Dexterity _____

    Precision _____

    Speed _____

    Verbal _____

    Versatility _____

Adapted from Missouri Restaurant Association

Form 3.7 (continued)

Mental:

    Education _____
    Job Knowledge
        Equipment and Tools _____
        Food and Beverage _____
        Service _____
        Sanitation _____
    Judgment, Logic _____
    Planning, Initiative _____

Characteristics:

    Extrovert / Introvert _____
    Aggressive / Submissive _____
    Team Worker / Independent / Leader _____
    Social Graces _____
    Emotional Stability _____
    Attentive to Detail _____
    Creative _____
    Articulate _____

Adapted from Missouri Restaurant Association

Form 3.8

JOB SPECIFICATION

Job Title: Host / Hostess	**Hours of Work:** 5:00 p.m. to 11:00 p.m.
A. Age:	Must be 21. May be called on to serve alcholic beverages.
B. Education:	The minimum education requirement is two years of high school. The person must be articulate *with grammatically correct English. The person* must be able to add, subtract, and multiply accurately.
C. Job Knowledge:	A minimum of six months successful experience as a wait person.
	Six months successful experience in a responsible supervisory job or demonstrated leadership potential.
	Ability to perform as a wait person, cashier, or bus person.
	Basic understanding of food, beverages, service, sanitation, and related equipment and tools.
D. Judgment:	Must be able to make quick and accurate judgments in the dining area.
E. Physical:	Health, strength, and endurance sufficient to spend 85 percent of time walking and standing without showing fatigue.
	Good posture, graceful carriage, neatness, and good taste in appearance.
	Meticulous in personal hygiene.
F. Skill:	Requires a high degree of manual dexterity, precision, and rapid but graceful movements in crowded dining room.
	Excellent hearing and vision.
	Sensitivity to the needs of guests.
	Good verbal and math skills.

Form 3.8 (continued)

G. Characteristics:	Requires an outgoing personality.
	Must be sufficiently aggressive to insist upon meticulous and rigid conformity and standards of service.
	Must demonstrate leadership ability with other dining room personnel.
	An awareness of the social graces needed for the gracious serving of food and beverages.
	Sufficient emotional stability to handle problems calmly, objectively, and without emotional involvement.
	Attentive to all the details required for excellent dining room service.
	Articulate with an ability to communicate effectively with both customers and staff.

Chapter 4

Company Standards

In chapter 3, we asked why you should spend time developing job standards. This same question should be answered about company standards. Why should you put into writing your way of doing business? Why should you publish these company standards?

One reason for writing down company policy is to demonstrate compliance with federal, state, and local laws. It is important to show your concern for sanitation, employee safety, accident and fire prevention, and nondiscriminatory employment and work practices. Another reason is to simplify daily management. Procedures explain how policies are carried out in daily operations. Procedure manuals simplify life and show the desire to train, coach, and support employees. You have a better chance with people believing this is a good place to work and making a commitment to help the organization achieve desired results. A third reason to develop policies is there is no need to make off-the-cuff decisions under pressure. Each established policy clarifies and strengthens your communication with employees. Everything is clear to everyone concerned.

We have three major topics in this chapter: the employee handbook, policy and procedures manual, and wage scale policy. The employee handbook puts into writing your personnel practices. It may be considered a contract between you and the people who accept employment with your company. An important part of policy and procedures are the procedures manuals for each job. You may also want established policy on the important topics of sanitation and safety with specified procedures and appropriate checklists to uphold the policy. Anything that occurs on a daily basis or is a recurring and repetitive situation is a good topic for a policy and procedures manual. Think through wage scale practices and establish competitive and fair policies, as money is important to the employee.

EMPLOYEE HANDBOOK

The employee handbook is a tool used as an avenue of communication between the company and the employee. It is important the employee understands employee obligations and those things the company assumes as obligations to the employee. Much of the material that is covered in the handbook will be explained verbally to the new employee during the orientation. The handbook allows the new person a chance to read and make clear in her own mind what is probably a confusing situation. In this era of regulation, it is necessary to put into writing policies, benefits, and responsibilities.

An employee handbook contains the company's personnel policies. Put into writing the policies that assure compliance with state and federal law. Equally important are the policies that contribute to the growth and development of human resources. If a policy does not help your operation or is not required by regulation, do not use it and do not put it in writing.

There are certain common elements in an employee manual. We have used categories listed by the Management School of the Wisconsin Restaurant Association. The four categories appropriate for an employee handbook are: opening statements, employee policies, house policies, and fringe benefits. We are using the same format used by the Wisconsin Restaurant Association, listing broad topics within each category containing two or three points to consider for that category. This is only a guide and not all topics may fit your establishment. The following is a suggested index for an employee handbook.

      EMPLOYEE HANDBOOK INDEX
      OPENING STATEMENTS
      History of the Company
      Basic Management Philosophy
      Employee Signature of Understanding and Acceptance
      STANDARD EMPLOYEE POLICIES
      Payroll Policies
      Supervision
      Work Schedules
      Holidays
      Break Time–Meal Time
      Dress Code–Uniform Requirements
      Employee Orientation
      STANDARD HOUSE POLICIES

Courtesy and Customer Service
Menu Knowledge
Complaint Handling
After Work Policies
Communications
Performance Review
Promotion and Transfer Opportunities
Sanitation
Saftey
Breakage and Errors
Security
Grounds for Dismissal
Ending Employment
FRINGE BENEFITS
Meals
Vacations
Sick Leave
Provisions of Uniforms
Group Insurance
Other Benefits

Opening Statements

History of the Company

Each employee likes to feel that he is a part of a special group. Telling the story of your restaurant helps him become familiar with new surroundings. Some of the following information might be included:

When business was started?
Why it was started?
Who owns it, and who are the customers?
How did it get its name, location?
What type of menu is used?
What makes your place special?
Where do you get your special food supplies?
Where do you get your recipes?
Any stories of famous customers or special awards received.

Basic Management Philosophy

This should reflect management's goals, what it feels about the restaurant, the customers, the people it hires. It should reflect the company's standard for treatment of employees, customers, and how work goals will be accomplished. Some of the points to be included in a philosophy statement are:

> Hiring the best people and helping employees develop.
>
> Treating people, employees, and customers with consideration and respect.
>
> Keeping a healthy and safe restaurant.
>
> Making employees members of a team and keeping team members informed of developments in the business.
>
> Providing service to the customers with enthusiasm.
>
> Serving a consistently high quality food and beverage product.
>
> Expecting everyone, employees and management, to do a good day's work.
>
> Making a commitment not to discriminate in hiring, training, or promotion on the basis of race, religion, sex, national origin, or handicap.

Employee Signature of Understanding and Acceptance

A simple statement indicating the employee has read the handbook and understands these policies are a condition of employment is needed. A signed statement should be part of the employee's permanent personnel file. Have a duplicate copy of this page so the employee will have a copy of the signed statement and the business can keep a copy on file.

Standard Employee Policies

Payroll Policies

It is important that the employee is clear about pay. The things that need to be understood usually include the following:

> When is payday?
>
> What pay period is reflected on the check?
>
> How does the employee receive the check and who gives out the checks?
>
> Who to ask if there is any question about the check.
>
> What all the numbers and information on the check stub mean.
>
> What is gross pay and what is net pay?

Exactly what are all the deductions and why the deductions are made.

The employee's responsibility to provide correct information.

How employee information is collected. What forms are used.

Any special circumstance that might occur such as, a lost check, garnishment of wages, or an advance on pay.

Supervision

Every employee must be clear on who gives orders and who to see with questions or problems. You may wish to illustrate this with an organization chart that shows who makes decisions for each area. Stress the important role of the immediate supervisor and ensure that employees realize the lines of communication are always open to higher management.

Work Schedules

This is a very important section of the handbook because employees must understand and comply with work schedules. The employee handbook should contain information about the following schedule items:

The restaurant hours of operation.
Who prepares the work schedule.
When the schedule is prepared, and how far in advance.
How the work schedule is determined.
When it is posted.
Where it is posted.
How to keep track of hours worked.
What the provisions are for changing the schedule, if necessary.

Within this section you should also include information about time clocks, absenteeism, tardiness, and overtime. Getting the work done is the most important consideration. When regular hours are necessary to get the work done, everyone should be required to comply. Remember that habits of poor attendance and tardiness start with one or two employees. If management does not seem concerned, other employees will develop careless attendance habits.

Stress the importance of notifying a supervisor in advance of any difficulty with reporting for work. If the employee may be required to work beyond the scheduled shift, be sure to state that possibility. If employees are allowed to switch shifts, develop a policy that reflects management interest and always ensures giving the best service to customers.

Holidays

Employees expect that certain days of the year are given special consideration. The most common policy for holiday pay is to pay the regular rate if the employee does not work. If the employee does work on a holiday, the pay is a higher rate, time-and-a-half or double time, often with a holiday bonus.

> The handbook should clearly spell out these things:
> Eligibility requirements for the employee to receive holiday pay.
> The list of paid holidays.
> The rate of pay.

Break Time—Meal Time

Schedule adequate break and meal time but maintain good customer service. It is important to have a fair distribution of rest periods so that all employees have the chance to take care of personal needs, such as smoking or phone calls. Things to consider and provide in the handbook are:

> When breaks are to be taken.
> Where breaks are taken and where meals are eaten.
> Who should be notified.
> How coverage of duties is handled.
> What may be eaten.

Dress Code—Uniform Requirements

A dress code may be established as long as it does not discriminate by sex. You may want to consider providing a uniform and providing laundering for the uniform. The employee handbook should include the following type of information:

> Hair: cleanliness, length, and restraints.
> Facial hair: length of beards and mustaches.
> Hands and nails: cleanliness.
> Daily bath and use of a deodorant.
> Make-up: tasteful and appropriate.

Jewelry: safe, tasteful, and appropriate.
Good posture.
Uniform: cleanliness.
Where the uniform is obtained.
Who is responsible for laundering.
Shoes: type, keeping shined and in good repair.
Inspection procedure: formal or informal.

Employee Orientation

Put in writing some of the things you told the employee on the first day that are not covered in another section of the handbook, such as the following:

Employee parking.
Entry and exit to building.
Employee lockers.
Answering the telephone.
Employee use of telephone.
Employee smoking.
Department meetings.
Illustration of the layout of the restaurant.
Description of the work areas.

Standard House Policies

Courtesy and Customer Service

The customer is the reason for livelihood and we can take pride in our ability to provide the customer with genuine personal service. Important points to cover in discussing customer relations are:

Basis of business is good service.
Smile.
Quality products.
Friendly, courteous, and efficient service.
Special promotional activities.

Menu Knowledge

It is not unusual for a restaurant to require that every employee be familiar with every menu item. The handbook should cover the following:

- Menu items.
- Items included with order.
- Food ingredients.
- Preparation methods.
- Tastings for employees.
- Plating and service.
- Where to find information about menu items.
- Introducing new menu items.

Complaint Handling

Complaints will happen and it is better to be prepared and know what to do. Stress teamwork. If complaints are handled well, an angry person may turn into a friend. Some typical complaints the employee should know how to handle are:

- The food is cold.
- The order is wrong.
- The food does not taste right.
- The bill is incorrect.
- The service has been poor.
- The customer becomes difficult and makes a scene.

Let the employee know she is part of a team and will be supported in efforts to work with difficult customers. Employees should know they can call on management when they are unable to satisfy a complaining customer.

After Work Policies

Many places have a policy for employees after work hours to keep the focus of the working staff on the customer. Some policies you may want to think about are the following:

- Are employees allowed in the work area when not on duty?
- Are employees allowed in the operation when not on duty?
- Are employees allowed in the operation in uniform when not on duty?

Communication

The employee handbook is one of many communication tools you will use with your employees. All of your communications stress the need for teamwork and taking pride in doing a good job. Let the employee know that two-way communication is a part of the way you do business.

The handbook can specify the following methods of communications the employee will experience:

Staff meeting.
Bulletin board.
One-to-one sessions with supervisors.
Open-door policy for management.
Newsletters.
Pay envelope messages.

Performance Review

A performance review is part of a constant effort to maintain good quality products and service, improve productivity, and develop human resources. The employee should be told the following:

There is a regular review.
When to expect a review.
Who performs the review.
What the basis of the review is, usually productivity, quality, safety, and attendance.
How the employee will be assisted to develop and improve skills.
Does the performance review influence pay?

Promotion and Job Transfer Opportunities

It is important the handbook states promotional opportunities honestly. If there is little opportunity for promotion, it is best not to include this in your handbook. Many small operations need people who are flexible and can perform a variety of duties. Being able to transfer to other jobs may help the employee develop and benefit the operation. If promotional opportunities exist or transfers are encouraged, some of the information the employee needs to know is the following:

How much time must be spent in one position before an employee is eligible for movement?

How do employees request another position?

What is the role of education, workshops, or seminars?

If a request is turned down, how will the employee be informed of the reasons?

What are the opportunities to develop skills?

Sanitation

It is not recommended to build a sanitation manual into your employee handbook. Emphasize the importance of strict sanitation procedures and tell the employee how sanitary procedures will be learned.

Safety

Safety procedures belong in another manual. Within the employee handbook, stress your interest in the safety of all employees at all times. Things that should be included are:

Every accident must be reported for proper record keeping.

Fire procedures; exits, calling the fire department, location, and use of fire extinguishers.

Breakage and Errors

Enlist the efforts of all employees to keep costs down. If you are going to make deductions for negligent breakage and arithmetic errors, the employee handbook is an important place to provide this information. You should check local laws for your responsibility. Some states require the employee sign consent for each deduction of this type. Most states expect you to make a reasonable effort to see breakage and mistakes do not occur. You may wish to consider a positive approach with an incentive reward for a certain number of checks handled without error or a certain number of hours handling breakable items without a mishap.

Security

Your employees should understand management does exert reasonable theft control over employees as a routine way of doing business. Points that may be covered in the employee manual are:

Employee entrance and exit.

Procedures for carrying packages from the building.

Employee parking.

Periodic locker inspections.

Unauthorized personnel are not permitted in the kitchen area.

Grounds for Dismissal

Be specific about the grounds for dismissal and be consistent in application. Some common grounds for dismissal are:

Rude treatment of customers.
Not following rules.
Theft.
Continued tardiness.
Absenteeism without reasonable explanation.
Drinking.
Drug use.

Ending Employment

The most common requirement is a two-week notice period. Employers promise a two-week notice of dismissal or layoff and employees are requested to give two-weeks notice of quitting.

Fringe Benefits

Meals

A restaurant has an advantage over other types of businesses because of the ability to offer meals as an employee benefit. Meal policy should be made clear to the employee in the employee handbook. Provide information about the following:

Price of a meal.
What menu items may be eaten and those that are not allowed for employee discount.
Number of meals allowed per shift.
Where meals are eaten.
When meals are eaten.
How the food is ordered and paid for.
What the policy is for beverages.

Vacations

The customary policy is one week's paid vacation after one year, two weeks after two years, and three weeks after four to six years. The vacation policy statement needs to include:

>How vacation time is accrued.
>When the vacation schedule is determined.
>Who is responsible for the vacation schedule.
>The criteria for picking specific dates.
>When during the year the vacation may be taken.
>How vacation pay for tipped employees is computed.
>Whether the employee may select an extra check instead of vacation time.

Sick Leave

Typical sick leave policy will allow an employee one day per month with pay. Some of the information to be included in an employee handbook is:

>When is an employee eligible for sick leave?
>How is sick leave accrued?
>Maximum number of days that can be accumulated.
>Will unused sick days result in a pay benefit?
>Importance of notifying the supervisor of an illness.
>Special policies for an illness that lasts beyond four days.

Provision of Uniforms

Generally, employees appreciate assistance with clothing required for the workplace. In the employee handbook, explain your policy for the provision of uniforms and the laundering or dry cleaning of the uniforms. Some of the points to be covered are:

>Where to obtain the uniform.
>What costs are involved.
>How to turn in uniform for laundry or dry cleaning.
>What is the buy back or return policy if the employee leaves.

Group Insurance

There are many different group insurance plans you may offer to your employees. The handbook should tell the employee what types of plans are available, eligibility requirements, and where to find information.

Other Benefits

You may offer other types of benefits for your employees. Some suggested ones are:

- Profit sharing.
- Retirement plans.
- Merit awards.
- Child care.
- Discounts on private parties.
- Authorized use of equipment.
- Transportation benefits.
- Language instruction.
- Tuition benefits.

POLICY AND PROCEDURES MANUAL

In order to establish policies, choose an overall plan that establishes goals and objectives for a three-year, five-year, or even a ten-year horizon. For example, a goal may be to have a business mix with 50 percent of income from lunch, 35 percent from dinner, and 15 percent from bar service. The menu policy that would follow from this goal would reflect popular lunch selections like salads, soups, finger foods, and sandwiches. Service policy may set a time limit for serving and turning a table to encourage two or three turns for lunch. Procedures are written that will enable the dining room personnel to provide the needed quick, efficient, and courteous service.

Write down policies and procedures that are common practice and are already established in your operation. By doing so, the employees will follow these practices and you will have consistent application of procedures.

When you are establishing policy and procedures that deal with day-to-day operations, try them out for a period of time. Keep records of their impact to see the procedures achieve the desired result. Make revisions if necessary and if a procedure does not work, do not use it.

Consult with people who have more experience or expertise than you. There are others who can help you develop procedures. For example, your local health department will help with a sanitation manual. The equipment suppliers can help develop operating manuals for the specific pieces of equipment within your operation. The local chapter of the National Restaurant Association can provide advice about national and local regulations. Suppliers can provide you with specific information about how to best handle their product. Product associations like the Coffee Council can provide you with training material for a specific commodity. Some of your older workers may be a source of good information about the best way to perform a unit of work. In fact, your employees will appreciate the recognition of their expertise and this will help establish a good working relationship with them.

A Policy and Procedures Manual will actually consist of several manuals. Each job title will have its own set of procedures. You will want to set up an order so that employees can easily find the appropriate procedure. The best way is to have a manual for those critical activities that everyone needs to know, for example, A Sanitation Manual or A Safety Manual. The other procedures will be divided into front of the house positions and back of the house positions.

For those of you who will be writing operations manuals on a computer, think about how information will be retrieved. Set up the main topics as files for the main directory like the following: employee handbook, kitchen operations, dining room operations, sanitation manual, and safety manual. Each main directory topic will have sub-directory titles. For example, kitchen may have cook, pantry, and dishroom.

Each of these sub-directories may be further divided to have a menu that lists the contents of each job procedures manual. Normally, a person will be searching for a single procedures sheet or an operations checklist. Make this a user-friendly search.

Procedures Manuals

Kitchen Operations

As explained in chapter 3, the job analysis is the foundation for job procedures manuals. When you go through the process of setting standards of performance for each unit of work, it is necessary to list reference materials that help the employee understand the performance standard. All of the material you developed to explain your performance requirements for each job (job procedures, layout plans, illustrations, and checklists) will make up the procedures manual for that job. Each job has a dozen or so units of work plus some critical activities like sanitation or customer relations. The job description lists the units of work in the sequence they are performed. This sequence, along with the critical activities for that job, makes a good index for the procedures manual. For example, the job procedures manual index for a cook may contain all or some of the following: an appearance and grooming checklist; a work station setup sheet; information on obtaining raw materials, supplies, and recipes; sheets for production schedules and equipment operation procedures; procedures for handling food orders; forms for portion control, and plating and holding procedures; a food report (prepared, sold, leftover, consumed); procedures for storing and using leftovers and closing the kitchen; a sanitation manual and checklist; and saftey checklist. Keep in mind that this is just a list of procedures that are common to many kitchens—each operation has its own specific needs. It is difficult to tell you which job procedures sheets you will need to write and therefore, it is important for you to develop job descriptions for the jobs in your operation.

Two other examples are the job procedures manual index for a dishwasher and a receiving and storing clerk. The index for a dishwasher may contain the following: checklists for appearance and grooming, dishmachine setup, sanitation, and safety; instructions for operating the dishmachine; an illustration of rack use and storage devices; procedures for scraping, sorting, racking, handling, and storing dishes; and a cleaning chemicals sheet.

A receiving and storing clerk index may contain the following: checklists for appearance and grooming, receiving, sanitation, and safety; procedures for opening the receiving area, and the storeroom; sheets for receiving, storeroom, and cooler and freezer storage procedures; list of procedures for requisitioning and issuing, delivering to the cook's station, delivering to the dining area, and closing; and a sanitation manual. These indexes are samples that you may use to develop your own.

Dining Room Operations

In chapter three, we gave you our example of a job description for a waiter/waitress. We will use that job description to illustrate a job procedures manual index for that job. Our job description of waiter/waitress requires the following job procedures manual index: checklists for dress and grooming, sanitation, safety, and customer relations; sheets for service station procedures, table setting layout, guest check procedures, plate preparation, tray service, wine/food, wine service, side work and check payment procedures, and equipment operation procedures; a menu policy guide; and a sanitation manual. Remember, this is an example. You must write a job description that fits your operation.

Another job procedures manual that will help you in the day-to-day operation of the front of the house is the manual for the bartender. A typical index for a bartender (according to our job description) is as follows: checklists for appearance and grooming, sanitation, and saftey; sheets for bar check, bar service, bar table service, check payment, cash register, equipment operations, and closing the bar procedures; information on setting up the bar, inventorying and requisitioning supplies, and using drink recipe cards; and a customer relations manual. To create a successful index, you must answer the question, "What procedures are needed to meet the objectives of my restaurant?"

A Sanitation Manual

This is a very important manual and should be written so the employees understand the causes of foodborne illness and the standards of sanitation you want for your establishment. You will want one manual that covers the total operation. The sections that apply to a particular job title will also be included in the procedures manual for that job title. The best way to ensure your sanitation standards are met is to have a sanitation checklist for each area of your operation.

A sanitation manual should be broken into the following seven sections:

1. Importance to the General Public;
2. Teamwork and Sanitation;
3. Principles of Food-borne Illness;
4. Personal Hygiene;
5. Food Preparation and Storage;
6. Entry, Foyer, and Dining Room; and
7. Ware Washing and Environmental Cleaning.

The following explanations contain important points that should be covered within the seven sections above. Self-inspection checklists that cover all the areas of a food service operation are also included. These checklists should be rewritten to apply to your particular operation.

Importance to the General Public

This topic requires a brief statement about the responsibility of the food service operator and the employees of the operation to serve wholesome food and beverages. The public expects a food service business will do everything possible to protect the health and well-being of the customer.

Teamwork and Sanitation

This topic emphasizes the fact that everyone in an operation must have sanitation as a priority. Some of the points to be covered are:

> The public looks at the operation as a whole.
> Everyone is affected by the reputation of the operation.
> Everyone should be concerned about sanitation.
> Help each other meet sanitation standards.
> Sanitation requires constant adherence to correct practices.

Principles of Food-borne Illness

Explain the causes of food-borne illness so the employees will understand the reasons for personal hygiene and sanitary food handling rules. Your local health department will be able to give you all the details of local regulations and local enforcement procedures. All food service operations must know the health department regulations in their own community. The topics that should be covered in this area are:

> Pathogenic Micro-organisms
> Conditions for growth: food, moisture, temperature between 45 and 140 F, neutral environment, air, time.
> Protection: keep bacteria from spreading, growing, and killing bacteria.
> Food-borne diseases: staph (staphylococcus) food poisoning, salmonella, clostridium perfringens, strep (streptococcal) infections, infectious hepatitis, trichinosis, botulism, and chemical poisoning.
> Prevention of food-borne disease: personal hygiene, the time and temperature rules for storage and holding food, food handling to prevent cross contamination, cleaning and sanitizing equipment, and rodent and insect control.

Personal Hygiene

The National Restaurant Association has a publication titled "Sanitation Self-Inspection Program for Food Service Operators" that is a guide for developing your own sanitation checklist. Within this publication, they also provide guidelines for the use of checklists.

The most important personal hygiene practice that should be stressed is proper handwashing. Forms 4.1 and 4.2 are copies of the two self-inspection checklists that apply to personal hygiene:

> Personal Safety
> Cleanliness of Service Personnel

Food Preparation and Storage

The self-inspection checklists should be tailored to meet the needs of your operation. Establish your manual to reflect the flow of food as it enters your operation, is stored, goes through preparation, is held for service, and is sent to the dining room as a finished product. We have included the following sanitation self-inspection checklists on Forms 4.3–4.12:

> Food and supplies receiving
> Dry stores
> Refrigerator storage
> Freezer storage
> Food handling practices
> Vegetable preparation
> Meat cutting area
> Baking area
> Food preparation and holding
> Vehicles used for transporting food

Entry, Foyer, and Dining Room

Try to approach this area from the view of the customer. The customer is forming an image of your establishment even as they park the car and walk toward your front door. Forms 4.13–4.18 are sanitation self-inspection checklists for the following areas:

> Entryways, exits and exterior surroundings
> Entrance foyer or waiting room
> General cleanliness of dining area
> Dining room and serving area
> Restrooms
> Sensory factors

Ware Washing and Environmental Cleaning

One of the best tools for sanitizing your operation is the dish washing machine. The procedures manual for the job of washing dishes should be carefully written. Within the sanitation manual develop checklists to ensure compliance with your sanitation standards and policy. Forms 4.19-4.23 may be used to develop guidelines for these areas:

> Ware washing and storage
> Garbage and trash storage and disposal areas
> Storage rooms for supplies and equipment
> Employee facilities
> Mechanical rooms

A Safety Manual

Many accidents are preventable. There are potentially hazardous conditions within the ordinary food service operation, but making your employees aware of hazards and stressing safe practices can prevent accidents from happening.

An index of topics for your safety maual should include the following seven sections:

1. Importance of Safety;
2. Employee Practices;
3. Food Preparation Areas;
4. Storage Areas;
5. Entryways and Dining Room;
6. Ware Washing; and
7. Fire Protection and Fire Prevention.

We have included fire protection and fire prevention as part of the safety manual. You may wish to treat this important subject with a separate manual.

The following lists the seven major topics covered in a safety manual with points to cover under each topic. The best way to ensure good accident and fire prevention procedures are followed is by using self-inspection checklists. Set up a safety manual for the total operation dividing it into back of the house and front of the house operations. The procedures manual for each unit of work will also include the appropriate checklist for safe working practices.

We are giving you checklists that are published by the National Restaurant Association and the U.S. Department of Health and Human Services. Use these checklists to develop checklists for your own operation.

Importance of Safety

Emphasize that you are personally interested in the safety of all employees at all times. Training for safety practices is part of the job training for all employees and all employees are expected to continue with safe working habits.

One of the ways to prevent accidents is to be aware of hazards. Ask the employees to inform you of potential safety hazards they see and take corrective measures within a reasonable time.

An accident is a stressful situation for everyone. Accidents are investigated to see if a safer working practice can be established that will prevent future accidents. Ask employees to report all accidents so that you may keep proper records and perform proper investigations.

Employee Practices

Some of the hazards that require an awareness of the need for safe behavior by the employees are:

    Handling knives.
    Handling hot food.
    Hot grease.
    Wet floors.

All employees need to know where first aid supplies are available and how to use them in a prudent manner. Checklist 4.1 is a self-inspection checklist for safe employee practices.

Food Preparation

In addition to safe employee practices, there are places in the preparation of food that can be potentially hazardous. Checklists 4.2–4.5 are self-inspection checklists for accident prevention in these areas:

    Floors
    Ventilation
    Electrical Equipment
    Food Preparation Area

Storage Areas

The correct way of lifting heavy objects, keeping storage areas orderly, and handling toxic materials properly are some of the safe working practices in the storage areas. Checklists 4.6–4.9 are accident prevention checklists for the following storage areas:

   Receiving area
   Storage areas
   Hazardous materials
   Waste storage area

Entryways and Dining Room

One of the responsibilities of the food service operator is to provide a safe place for customers. Some of the precautions that will help protect customers as well as employees are identified in the accident prevention Checklists 4.10–4.13:

   Doors and exits
   Stairs, ramps, and ladders
   Serving area and dining room
   Lighting

Ware Washing

Wet floors and hot temperatures make this a potentially hazardous area. The following two checklists are included to enable you to develop accident prevention checklists for your operation (checklists 4.14–4.15):

   Utensil washing area
   Hot water heating

Fire Protection and Fire Prevention

Fire protection and fire prevention are part of job training activities. They are critical areas that should be the priority of everyone in the establishment. Sanitary practices, accident prevention, and fire prevention are all closely related. Keeping a place clean and safe helps to eliminate fire hazards.

Even though fire drills and emergency procedures are given in training sessions, put them in writing. Keep these written emergency procedures in a place known to all employees, one that is easily located during an emergency. Employees should know who

Checklist 4.1

EMPLOYEE PRACTICES

Are all employees aware of hazards existing in their work areas?

Are employees properly instructed on placement of hands to avoid injury when handling potentially hazardous devices such as slicers?

Do employees make use of all guards, hot pads, railings, and other protective devices available to them?

Do employees wear proper shoes that are nonskid and will protect feet from injury?

Do employees wear clothing that cannot get caught in mixers, cutters, grinders, fans, or other equipment?

Is at least one employee on each shift trained in emergency first aid techniques?

Checklist 4.2

FLOORS

Are all floors in safe condition—free from broken tile and defective floorboards, worn areas, and items that may cause people to trip or fall?

Are spills and debris removed from the floor immediately?

Where floors are frequently wet, are heavy traffic areas provided with nonskid mats?

Are floors mopped adequately and provided with a protective or nonskid finish to prevent slipping?

Are adequate floor drains provided and properly covered with gratings?

Are all carpets securely tacked or otherwise fastened in place to prevent people from tripping over raised edges?

Company Standards

Checklist 4.3

VENTILATION

Is the ventilation adequate in receiving, storage, and dishwashing areas and in walk-in coolers and freezers?

Are vent filters and fresh-air intakes provided in food-preparation, serving, and dining areas?

Are all fans and their moving parts shielded or guarded?

Is gas equipment properly vented?

Checklist 4.4

ELECTRICAL EQUIPMENT

Is electrical equipment properly grounded, wired, and fused?

Is electrical equipment of approved type and installed properly?

Does it meet the National Electrical Code specifications or local ordinances and bear the seal of the Underwriter's Laboratories?

Are regular inspections of equipment and wiring made by an electrician?

Are electrical switches readily accessible in emergencies?

Are switches located so that employees do not have to lean on or against metal when reaching for them?

Are cords maintained without splices, cracks, or worn areas?

Is wiring kept off floors and surfaces subject to vibration, and out from under equipment?

Is electrical equipment protected against the entrance of water?

Are weatherproofed cords and plugs provided for outdoor equipment?

Are wet floors and areas subject to flooding avoided for placement of electrical equipment?

Are protective pads or platforms provided for people to stand on who use or vend from machines?

Are service cords long enough to eliminate the need for extension cords?

Are all switches, junction boxes, and outlets covered?

Does all equipment with cord and plug connections have grounded connections—either three-pronged plugs or pigtail adapters?

Checklist 4.5

FOOD PREPARATION AREA

Are prepared foods properly protected from contamination from above?

Is adequate aisle space provided between equipment to allow reasonable work movement and traffic?

Is a nonsplintering, easily cleanable tamper provided for use with grinders?

Are hot pads, asbestos gloves, spatulas, or other equipment provided for use with stoves, ovens, and other hot equipment?

Are scabbards, sheaths, racks, or magnetic bars available for proper storage of knives and other sharp instruments?

Are machines properly guarded?

Do employees make use of tampers, hot pads, safe knife storage devices, and machine guards provided for their protection?

Are knives and other blades kept sharp?

Are employees properly instructed in the operation of machines, mixers, grinders, choppers, dishwashers, and so forth?

Are cooking utensil handles always positioned so that they do not protrude over the edges of cooking units and into passageways?

If anything breaks near the food preparation or service area, are workers trained to discard all food from the areas adjacent to the breakage to prevent contamination?

Are stoves, vent filters, and cooking areas properly cleaned to remove greases and flammable wastes?

Are mixers in safe operating condition? Are beaters properly maintained to avoid introducing bits of metal and other foreign particles into the food?

Are steam tables regularly maintained by competent personnel?

If the temperature of the kitchen is very high, are employees aware of the symptoms of heat strain?

Company Standards

Checklist 4.6
RECEIVING AREA

Are employees instructed in correct opening, lifting, and storing methods for each item that is received?

Checklist 4.7
STORAGE AREAS

Is there sufficient space for storage of everything, with nothing stored on floors, in corridors, or on stairways?

Are shelves located and constructed to prevent pinched fingers?

Are shelves adequate to bear the weight of the items stored?

Are heavy items stored on lower shelves and lighter materials above?

Is a safe ladder or step stool provided for reaching high shelves?

Are portable storage racks and stationary racks in safe condition, free from broken or bent shelves and standing solidly on legs?

Is there a safety device in the walk-in cooler to permit exit from the inside, and a light switch inside?

Is the refrigerant in the refrigerator nontoxic? (Check with repairperson.)

Checklist 4.8
HAZARDOUS MATERIALS

Are toxic materials and hazardous substances properly stored and handled?

Are cylinders of explosive gas secured or strapped to prevent their falling or rolling?

Are combustible and flammable materials stored and handled properly?

Are compressed carbon dioxide tanks stored properly in a cool, dry, well-ventilated, and fire resistant area? Are they protected from falling over? Are pressure gauges on the tanks working?

Are cartons or other flammable materials stored far enough away from light bulbs and other sources of heat?

Checklist 4.9

WASTE STORAGE AREA

Are garbage and waste containers constructed of leak-proof material?

Are garbage containers covered when not in use?

Are containers adequate in number and size?

Are containers cleaned frequently?

Are disposal area floors and surroundings kept clean and clear of refuse?

Is there a proper rack for holding garbage containers?

Are containers on dollies, or other wheeled units, to eliminate lifting by employees?

Checklist 4.10

DOORS AND EXITS

Are sidewalks and entrance and exit steps kept clean and in good repair?

Will all exits open from the inside without keys to allow escape from the building?

Can an exit be reached from every point in the building without having to pass through an area of high potential hazard?

Are routes to exits, and the exits themselves, clearly marked?

Are passages to exits kept free of equipment and materials?

Are all exits outward opening?

Are doors hung so they do not open into passageways where they could cause accidents?

Checklist 4.11

STAIRS, RAMPS, AND LADDERS

Are stairs and slopes clearly marked and illuminated?

Do stairs have abrasive surfaces to prevent slipping and falling?

Are handrails on open sides of stairways provided?

Are center handrails provided for wide stairs?

Are stairways kept unobstructed?

Is there a 7-foot clearance over each step?

Are the slopes of ramps set to provide maximum safety and are not too steep?

Are ladders maintained in good condition and inspected frequently?

Do ladders have nonslip bases?

Checklist 4.12

SERVING AREA AND DINING ROOM

Are serving counters and tables free of broken parts, wooden or metal slivers, and sharp edges or corners?

Is all tableware regularly inspected for chips, cracks, or flaws? Are defective pieces discarded in a safe manner?

Is the traffic flow coordinated to prevent collisions while people are carrying trays or obtaining food?

Are pictures and wall decorations securely fastened to walls?

Are ceiling fixtures firmly attached and in good repair?

Checklist 4.13

LIGHTING

Is lighting adequate in all areas?

Are light fixtures, bulbs, tubes, and so forth, protected with screen guards?

Is proper heat-proof lighting provided over cooking areas, in vent hoods, and so forth?

Checklist 4.14

UTENSIL WASHING AREA

If conveyor units are used to move soiled items, are edges guarded to avoid catching fingers or clothing?

Are portable racks or bus trucks in safe operating condition—wheels and castors working, shelves firm?

Are dish racks kept off the floor to prevent people from tripping and falling over them?

Is there an adequate drainboard or other drying area so that employees do not pile pots and pans on the floor?

Are racks, hooks, and gloves provided so that dishwashers do not have to put their hands into sanitizing baths of hot water or chemicals?

Are drain plugs mechanically operated or provided with chains so that employees can drain sinks without placing hands in sanitizing hot water?

Checklist 4.15

HOT WATER HEATING

Are safety devices, such as temperature and pressure relief valves, or energy cutoffs, provided to prevent explosion of pressurized water heating systems?

Do safety valves meet the standards of the American Standards Association or the American Society of Mechanical Engineers?

Is hot water temperature properly controlled in lavatories and sinks or are mixing faucets provided to prevent scalding?

Are backflow preventers installed wherever necessary?

Are overhead pipes or fixtures high enough to prevent head bumping?

is to call the fire department, the telephone number, and evacuation procedures. Directions for use of fire extinguishers should be clearly and plainly posted.

Checklists for self-inspection for fire prevention are published by the National Restaurant Association. Use these checklists to develop appropriate checklists for your own operation. These fire prevention checklists should also be included in each work unit procedures manual. Forms 4.24–4.30 are fire prevention checklists.

DEVELOPING WAGE PLAN POLICY

Often our long-term goals and the criteria we use to judge success involve our financial resources. Some of our long-term goals may be to pay off a debt, buy a building, buy property, earn a living, or support our family. Our objectives are often stated in dollar amounts, food sales, bar sales, carry-out sales, profit, investment return, gross income, and net income. In a food service business, a lot of time is spent setting up plans for how we will use food commodities. Recipes, menus, and production schedules are all important to our business. Money is also important and we need to spend time planning how to best use this important resource.

A critical use of this important resource is to buy the labor needed to produce our products and serve our customers. When we are developing policy for our business, wage policy is too important to be left to the decisions of government legislators or the plans of our competitors. While this section does not directly tell you how to train employees, it does give you some ideas that will show your employees you are trying to be fair. This can set the stage for your employees to want to learn.

Job Classification and Pay Scales

Good employee relations cannot be established by wages alone but a sound pay plan helps to improve the working environment. It is important to the employee that they see the pay rates as fair and equitable within the business. It is disturbing to employees to see what they consider unfair differences in pay within their group.

All of the intricacies of compensation plans are beyond the elements of a book on training. However, the analysis you perform to set up training systems is the starting point for developing sound pay plans. We want to show you a way to develop different levels of jobs that will help you think about equitable pay scales. We will use the Job Specification Worksheet (Form 4.31) to set up a point system for judging the value of a job to the enterprise. The point system for evaluating jobs for the purpose of setting equitable wages involves four steps:

1. A yardstick is set up with a set of factors against which each job can be evaluated. Each factor has a number of degrees with each degree worth a number of points.

2. A job specification is written indicating the importance of each factor.

3. Each job is rated for each factor and a point value is assigned.

4. The point value puts the job into a job classification and a wage is assigned.

Using the 36 factors listed on the Job Specification Worksheet (for example, age, appearance, strength, endurance), each factor will have four degrees. Basic, which means the person meets a basic standard, has a value of one point. Competent, which means the person is able to perform well and is fully trained, is worth two points. Leads/trains means the position requires leadership in this factor or the person is able to explain and train others in the skill. It is worth three points. Solves problems/creates means the person can solve problems or create solutions that improve performance, create product improvements, or create promotional activities. This factor enhances the business and is worth four points.

In order to assign a point value, rank the importance of the five categories to your operation. Skill factors probably have a greater value to your business than personal requirements. For our example, we are assigning the following weights to each category: Personal Requirements 10 percent, Posture 10 percent, Skill 30 percent, Mental 25 percent, and Characteristics 25 percent. These numbers will serve as multipliers for the factor scores and will give you point values that reflect the importance of the category to your operation. We are using these numbers as an example. You should set the relative value of each area according to the needs of your own operation.

Now take each job and assign a degree number to each factor. Form 4.32 shows the degree points assigned to each factor for a hostess. Form 4.33 also shows the degree numbers for a dishwasher. To make the calculation, it is necessary to consider the total points possible for each category and determine the ratio of the score to the total possible. The hostess score in our example is 14 points out of 24 possible for Personal Requirements. Write this 14/24 and figure the ratio of 14/24 to equal .583. Make the same calculation for each category: Posture 11/32 = .344, Skill 18/28 = .643, Mental 19/28 = .678, and Characteristics

22/32 = .687. Each ratio is multiplied by the weighing numbers given to each category:

.583 x 10 = 5.83
.344 x 10 = 3.44
.643 x 30 = 19.29
.678 x 25 = 16.95
.687 x 25 = *17.17*
Total = 62.68

The total 62.68 is the point value for the hostess job. The comparison is made with the point value of other jobs. Those jobs that fall into higher point values should be assigned a higher pay scale. The calculations for the dishwasher's job show a point value of :

.416 x 10 = 4.16
.437 x 10 = 4.37
.393 x 30 = 11.79
.357 x 25 = 8.92
.312 x 25 = *7.8*
Total = 37.04 (dish washer job point value)

As you calculate the point value for all your jobs, they will fall into different levels. You will usually have four or five distinct levels. Wage rates can be assigned for each level. Frequently, a range of pay rates is assigned to each job level. For each job level you may also want to assign a starting pay rate, job rate, and merit rate. The job rate may also have a range of rates that depend upon seniority. When the top job rate is reached, then wage increases will only be for cost-of-living. Set a criteria for merit increases based upon real increases in value for the business.

Incentive Pay

When you were writing the job description, we suggested you may wish to give certain items a high priority rating. We will give you an example of how you can set up a system that rewards the employee for superior performance in those categories you judge are most critical to the success of your restaurant. It involves the assignment of point values for the importance of the item and the level of performance.

We will use the job description from chapter three for waiter/waitress on Form 4.34. Each duty is assigned a point value based on its importance to the job as a whole. These point values add up to 100 percent—the total job. A different set of point values is used to weigh each level of performance: three points for superior, two points for competent, one point for minimum, and zero for below minimum. After evaluating each item, multiply the two point values. Then add the results to give you an overall performance rating. Rewards can then be based on point scores; the people with the highest scores get the rewards (Miller & Porter, 1985). When employees are rewarded in this system, it is based upon their own job, not a comparison with a different job.

External Factors

Federal Minimum Wage Law

In the real world in which we do business, our wage rates are heavily influenced by external factors. The federal government and some states have a minimum wage law. Employers need to follow the laws that apply to their operation. The federal minimum wage law passed in 1989 has the following provisions:

1. The law provides for a sub-minimum wage for 16- to 19-year-old workers during the first 90 days of employment. An employee could then be paid the sub-minimum wage by the employer for an additional 90 days only if the employee is participating in an on-the-job training program that meets Department of Labor requirements.

2. The sub-minimum wage would be $3.35 an hour (the current minimum wage) between April 1, 1990 and March 31, 1992, and then 85 percent of the regular minimum wage, or $3.61 an hour. This sub-minimum wage will terminate on April 1, 1993.

3. As it presently stands, the Department of Labor will have no direct role in certifying the training programs that employers must institute in order to qualify to pay participant employees the sub-minimum wage for three additional months (90 days). In order to meet the new law, however, employers will annually be required to notify the Department of Labor that they have a training wage for specified jobs, maintain a written plan on the premises, post a notice identifying that the plan is in existence, and provide eligible employees with a copy of the plan. (The plans will have to meet criteria that the Department of Labor will publish before April 1, 1990—the first date the minimum wage increase becomes effective.)

4. On-the-job training plans will be reviewed and scrutinized for consistency with the criteria to be specified by the Department of Labor during compliance investigations conducted by the Wage and Hour Division of the Department of Labor.

5. The new law requires two annual increases of 45 cents each for employees. Accordingly, effective April 1, 1990, employees must be paid $3.80 and, effective April 1, 1991, $4.25 an hour (Foster, 1989).

Competition

Each business must decide the competitive level of its pay scale. Businesses set a wage policy to pay wages that are high, average, or below average. Some of the factors to consider when making the policy decision are: recruitment and selection needs, employment conditions in the area, need for a good public image, the influence of unions, the business's economic condition, and other factors such as the seasonal nature of the business, the rate of inflation, and fringe benefits.

Fringe Benefits

A certain amount of wage benefits will be used for things other than pay. An attractive fringe benefit package can be an asset for recruiting capable employees. Since most food service operations have limited resources a creative problem-solving approach for determining fringe benefits may be helpful. Use the same three questions used in Chapter 2 when we were looking for ways to overcome barriers to employment. These questions were: What government or community resources are available?; How can company resources be used? and How can employees be helped to help themselves?

The last question points out that employees will appreciate input about the fringe benefit program. Keep the program flexible enough that the individual employee will have some choices as to which benefits will be most appropriate for her situation.

Health Insurance

One of the most difficult problems for companies or workers with limited resources is health care insurance. Investigate what plans are available to you and how they fit your financial picture. Your local chapter of the Restaurant Association is a good source of information for what is available in your community. Also investigate what type of preventive health care options are available in your community. Most communities offer free or low cost diagnostic services such as hearing exams or cholesterol testing. Many communities have health care fairs where health care professionals will provide free or low cost information. Encourage your employees to take advantage of community health service programs. Health insurance plans and benefits can be complex and confusing to your employees. Ask the insurance carrier to help you explain the features and benefits of their plan to your employees.

Meals

As a food service professional you are able to offer your employees an expertise on the selection of healthful food items. A healthy diet is an excellent way to practice preventive medicine. Remember the restaurant has an advantage over other businesses in its ability to offer meals as fringe benefits.

Retirement and Profit Sharing

In your efforts to acquire ownership of a food service operation, you have learned the importance of having capital assets. This is another area of expertise that can be shared with your employees. Two areas where it is possible to provide an opportunity for your workers to acquire some capital assets are the IRA and profit sharing plans.

Child Care

One other fringe benefit that has been gaining popularity in recent years is the provision of child care for employees. See what is available within your community and whether it would be suitable for your workers. If you do not have the resources to set up a child care facility, perhaps a cooperative effort with other small businesses would be appropriate. Remember many child care professionals are themselves small business owners and appreciate the need for the careful use of financial resources.

Summary

Wage policy is one of those areas where you want to reflect sound management. You do not want to make irrational, off-the-cuff decisions under pressure that can set a precedent you may have to live with for a long time. Your goal is to be fair to your employees and to yourself.

REFERENCES

Miller, Jack E. and Mary Porter. 1985. *Supervision in the Hospitality Industry*. New York: John Wiley and Sons, p. 183.

National Restaurant Association. 1983. *Sanitation Self-Inspection Program*. Washington, DC: National Restaurant Association. This pamphlet provides excellent directions for developing a self-inspection program and provides checklists.

National Restaurant Association. *Fire Protection and Fire Prevention*. Washington, DC: National Restaurant Association. This pamphlet covers food service fires with material about fire extinguishers, fire prevention and fire protection programs, fire insurance, and self-inspection checklists.

Strauss, George and Leonard R. Sayles. 1972. *Personnel: The Human Problems of Management*. Englewood Cliffs, NJ: Prentice-Hall, Inc. pp. 556-560.

U.S. Department of Health and Human Services. *Health and Safety Guide for Eating and Drinking Places*. DHEW Publication No. (NIOSH) 76-163. This government publication provides help for complying with OSHA regulations.

Wisconsin Restaurant Association. 1976. *A Manual for Writing Your Employee Handbook*. Wisconsin Restaurant Association Management School. This manual was printed in connection with a workshop presented by the Wisconsin Restaurant Association. It has a logical format for preparing the employee handbook and contains points of consideration for each topic.

Form 4.1

PERSONAL SAFTEY (Infections and illness, hygiene, and grooming)

Date Inspected: _____   **Inspected by:** _____

Item	Y	N	Comments on Deficiencies and Action Required	Date Corrected
Do food handlers have infected burns, cuts, boils?				
Do food handlers have acute respiratory illness?				
Do food handlers have infections or contagious illness transmittable through foods?				
Are food handlers wearing clean outer garments?				
Are food handlers free of body odors?				
Are food handlers' hands clean—washed at start of work day and as frequently as necessary?				
Are food handlers wearing hats, caps or hair nets, or other effective hair restraints?				
Are food handlers observed picking nose or pimples, scratching head or face?				
Are food handlers observed smoking or eating in food preparation or serving areas?				
Are fingernails of food handlers short and clean?				

Reprinted by permission of the National Restaurant Association

Company Standards

Form 4.1 (continued)

Item	Y	N	Comments on Deficiencies and Action Required	Date Corrected
Are instances of spitting in sinks, on floor, or in disposal area observed?				
Are food servers seen to cough in hands?				
Are food handlers wearing rings (other than plain band), dangling bracelets, wristwatches, etc., while preparing or handling food?				
Are cloths used to wipe off perspiration on face used for no additional purpose?				
Have all employees been instructed on minimum sanitation and food protection requirements?				

Form 4.2

CLEANLINESS OF SERVICE PERSONNEL

Date Inspected:_____   Inspected by:_____

Item	Y	N	Comments on Deficiencies and Action Required	Date Corrected
Are waitress uniforms wrinkled or soiled?				
Do service personnel use strong perfume or smell of body odor?				
Are servers sniffing, coughing, or rubbing or wiping nose?				
Do servers handle drinking glasses by their tops or silverware by their blades, tines, or bowls?				
Are servers using effective hair restraints?				
Do cooks and servers smoke in view of customers?				
Do servers handle rolls butter, ice, etc., by hand in filling dishes and water glasses?				
Do employees scratch head, face, or body in view of customers?				
Do servers touch food with thumbs or fingers when serving plated food?				

Reprinted by permission of the National Restaurant Association

Company Standards   4-39

Form 4.3

FOOD AND SUPPLIES RECEIVING

Date Inspected: _____   **Inspected by:** _____

Item	Y	N	Comments on Deficiencies and Action Required	Date Corrected
Is food inspected immediately upon receipt for spoilage or infestation?				
Is perishable food promptly moved to refrigeration?				
Are unattended perishable food deliveries on loading dock or dolly?				
Are nonfood supplies checked for infestation?				
Are empty shipping containers and packing promptly removed to disposal area?				
Is receiving area free of food particles and debris?				
Is floor of receiving area clean?				
Are packages dated upon receipt to assure "first-in-first-out" use?				
Are shellfish packages identified with processor's or packer's name and number?				

Reprinted by permission of the National Restaurant Association

Form 4.4

DRY STORES

Date Inspected: _____   **Inspected by:** _____

Item	Y	N	Comments on Deficiencies and Action Required	Date Corrected
Is all food stores at least six inches off the floor—on shelves, racks or platforms?				
Is the floor clean and free from spilled food?				
Are shelves high enough off floor to permit cleaning underneath, or is area beneath shelf enclosed to preclude accumulation of soil?				
Are shelves away from wall to permit ventilation and discourage nesting of insects and rodents?				
Have empty cartons and trash been removed?				
Are canned goods moved from cartons to shelving to extent practicable?				
Are food storage shelves clean and free of dust and debris?				
Are food supplies stored in a manner to ensure "first-in-first-out" use?				
Is storeroom dry—free from dampness?				
Are nonfood supplies stored separately from food stock?				

Reprinted by permission of the National Restaurant Association

Company Standards 4-41

Form 4.4 (continued)

Item	Y	N	Comments on Deficiencies and Action Required	Date Corrected
Are all toxic materials (including pesticides) labeled and used from only original containers?				
Are pesticides stored in a separate well-marked cabinet?				
Is there evidence of insects or rodents?				
Is there evidence of misuse or spillage of insecticides or rodenticides?				
Are bulk foods (sugar, flour), if no longer stored in original package, now stored in a covered container with identifying name?				
Are food and containers stored under exposed or unprotected sewer or water lines or close to "sweating" walls?				
Are most frequently needed items on lower shelves and near entrance?				
Are heavy packages stored on lower shelves?				

Form 4.5

REFRIGERATOR STORAGE

Date Inspected:_____   Inspected by:_____

Item	Y	N	Comments on Deficiencies and Action Required	Date Corrected
Are refrigerators equipped with accurate thermometers located in warmest part of cabinet?				
Are all refrigerators operating and maintaining potentially hazardous foods at temperatures of 45°F or lower?				
Are refrigerators clean and free from mold and objectionable odors?				
Is all potentially hazardous food, not in actual preparation or hot holding, stored under refrigeration?				
Is all food being stored off the floor of walk-in refrigerators?				
Are foods stored on shelves spaced to provide for adequate air circulation, and is shelving free of linings that retard circulation?				
Are panned, raw, or cooked foods on shelves, covered to prevent contamination?				
Are cooked foods such as ground meat, stew, dressing, or gravy not stored in large quantity containers?				

Reprinted by permission of the National Restaurant Association

Company Standards

Form 4.5 (continued)

Item	Y	N	Comments on Deficiencies and Action Required	Date Corrected
Are foods stored in a manner to permit "first-in-first-out" use?				
Is proper cleaning and maintenance being conducted?				
Are any spoiled foods present?				
Are raw foods stored separately from cooked foods?				
Are shelves high enough from the floor to permit cleaning underneath?				
Are shelves free from food husks, leaves, wrapping, or debris?				
Are there sufficient refrigeration facilities to handle normal delivery shcedules?				
Is there sufficient space in the refrigerators to permit good air circulation around the stored food?				
Is there awareness that ice used for cooling will not be used for human consumption?				
Are solid cuts of meat (except quarters and sides) covered in storage and placed to allow circulation of cool air?				
Are cooked foods or other products removed from original containers, put in clean, sanitized, covered containers, and identified?				

Form 4.5 (continued)

Item	Y	N	Comments on Deficiencies and Action Required	Date Corrected
Are dairy products stored separately from strong-odor foods?				
Are fish stored apart from other food products?				

Company Standards

Form 4.6

FREEZER STORAGE

Date Inspected: _____   **Inspected by:** _____

Item	Y	N	Comments on Deficiencies and Action Required	Date Corrected
Are freezer storage units operating?				
Do all boxes or cabinets have accurate thermometers?				
Are freezer storage units maintaining an interior temperature of 0°F, or lower?				
Is there excessive traffic in and out of walk-in freezer storage boxes?				
Is food stored in a manner to ensure air circulation?				
Is food stored in a manner that permits "first-in-first-out" use?				
Do cabinet walls or coils need defrosting?				
Are foods wrapped well to prevent freezer burn?				
Are all food containers covered?				
Is proper cleaning and maintenance being conducted?				

Reprinted by permission of the National Restaurant Association

Form 4.7

FOOD HANDLING PRACTICES

Date Inspected: _____   **Inspected by:** _____

Item	Y	N	Comments on Deficiencies and Action Required	Date Corrected
Is food in pans or containers on floor?				
Are perishable or potentially hazardous foods being held at room temperature?				
Are fruits and vegetables thoroughly washed prior to preparation and serving?				
Are food warmers, steam tables, and bainmaries used to reheat prepared foods?				
Are frozen foods being properly thawed under refrigeration or under cold running water or being cooked directly from frozen state?				
Are raw and cooked ready-to-serve foods being prepared on the same cutting board without washing and sanitizing the board between changed use?				
Are hands being used to pick up rolls, bread, butter pats, ice, or other foods to be served?				

Reprinted by permission of the National Restaurant Association

Company Standards

Form 4.7 (continued)

Item	Y	N	Comments on Deficiencies and Action Required	Date Corrected
Are waitresses or busboys handling place settings and serving food without washing hands after wiping tables and busing solied dishes?				
Are food servers touching food contact surfaces of plates, tumblers, cups, and silverware when setting table or serving customer?				

Form 4.8

VEGETABLE PREPARATION

Date Inspected:_____   Inspected by:_____

Item	Y	N	Comments on Deficiencies and Action Required	Date Corrected
Is the vegetable preparation area clean and free from objectionable dampness and odor?				
Are nonrefrigerated vegetables stored in ventilated bins or in crates on elevated platforms?				
Is area free from empty containers and debris?				
Is vegetable sink(s) used for hand washing or for ware-washing?				
Is vegetable sink used for dumping mop water or pan drippings?				
Are peelers or paring knives present in vegetable sink?				
Are vegetable preparation equipment parts washed in the vegetable sink?				
Are vegetable peelers, slicers, choppers, etc., that are not in use clean?				
Are vegetable peelers, slicers, choppers, etc., being cleaned between changed use?				

Reprinted by permission of the National Restaurant Association

Company Standards

Form 4.9

MEAT CUTTING AREA

Date Inspected: _____   **Inspected by:** _____

Item	Y	N	Comments on Deficiencies and Action Required	Date Corrected
Is meat cutting area clean and free from objectionable odor, cartons, and other debris?				
Are meat cutting wastes discarded into approved containers and removed to the disposal area?				
Are cutting boards in good condition—free from splits, holes, or cuts?				
Are cutting boards cleaned and sanitized between changed use?				
Are all cutting boards, tables, grinders, slicers, meat saws, boning knives, and other meat cutting equipment clean and sanitized if not in use?				
Is raw meat awaiting preparation or processed meat cuts in containers, off the floor?				
Is raw meat awaiting processing or processed cuts being held for excessive periods at room temperature?				
Is frozen meat, poultry, or fish being thawed with warm water?				

Reprinted by permission of the National Restaurant Association

Form 4.10

BAKING AREA

Date Inspected:_____   Inspected by:_____

Item	Y	N	Comments on Deficiencies and Action Required	Date Corrected
Is baking area clean, dry, and free from empty cartons and debris?				
Are flour and other non-perishable bakery food ingredients off the floor and, if in other than original containers, properly marked?				
Are dough mixers, kettles, and other bakery equipment and utensils that are not in use clean?				
Are mixing bowls, pots, and other bakery utensils stored in a manner to prevent splattering and contamination?				
Are potentially hazardous bakery ingredients and unbaked fillings and liquid mixes not held at room temperature longer than absolutely necessary during preparation?				
Are pie fillings not being held and cooled in stock pots or other large containers and at room temperature?				
Are pesticides or cleaning supplies not stored or present in the bakery area?				

Reprinted by permission of the National Restaurant Association

Company Standards

Form 4.11

FOOD PREPARATION AND HOLDING

Date Inspected:_____   **Inspected by:**_____

Item	Y	N	Comments on Deficiencies and Action Required	Date Corrected
Is food preparation area generally clean and free from accumulated debris?				
Is floor of kitchen and other food preparation and service areas clean and dry?				
Is food preparation equipment not in use clean?				
Are utensils not in use clean, sanitized, and stored in a manner that will protect them from contamination?				
Is preparation equipment cleaned and sanitized between changed use? (This especially pertains to grinders, slicers, choppers and mixers, and knives.)				
Are cleaning supplies and pesticides present in the food preparation and service areas?				
Is cook's sink being used for employee hand washing or dumping of mop water?				
Is unused equipment or utensils stored behind ranges, ovens, or in other floor spaces in the kitchen area?				

Reprinted by permission of the National Restaurant Association

Form 4.11 (continued)

Item	Y	N	Comments on Deficiencies and Action Required	Date Corrected
Is there evidence of rodents or insects in the kitchen or serving lines of the establishment?				
Are thermostats operating and accurate on ranges and deep fat fryers?				
Is hot-holding equipment maintaining food at or above 140°F?				
Are cold foods being held at 45°F or lower and are cabinets equipped with thermometers?				

Company Standards

Form 4.12

VEHICLES USED FOR TRANSPORTING FOOD

Date Inspected: _____   **Inspected by:** _____

Item	Y	N	Comments on Deficiencies and Action Required	Date Corrected
Is the cargo area of the vehicle thoroughly clean and free from dirt and debris?				
Has all food in containers been removed for proper disposal or storage?				
Is potentially hazardous food being carried at proper temperatures of heat or cold?				
Is food being carried in adequately insulated containers?				
Are all food spills on shelving or floor washed from the vehicle after each use?				
Is there any evidence of insect infestation on the vehicle body?				

Reprinted by permission of the National Restaurant Association

Form 4.13

ENTRYWAYS, EXITS, AND EXTERIOR SURROUNDINGS (Including parking lots and drive-in service area)

Date Inspected: _____   **Inspected by:** _____

Item	Y	N	Comments on Deficiencies and Action Required	Date Corrected
Are entryways clear of trash and debris?				
Are doors, windows, and screens tight-fitting to prevent entry of insects and rodents?				
Is there any evidence of rat holes or entry points near or into the building?				
Are there wet spots, pools, or long grass or weeds that could form breeding spots for insects?				
Is the parking lot or surrounding area free of litter, trash, and debris?				
Do noxious birds nest or roost on ledges or eaves of the establishment?				

Reprinted by permission of the National Restaurant Association

Company Standards 4-55

Form 4.14

ENTRANCE AND FOYER OR WAITING ROOM

Date Inspected:_____   Inspected by:_____

Item	Y	N	Comments on Deficiencies and Action Required	Date Corrected
Is the entryway and waiting room clean and attractive?				
Is it free from litter?				
Are chairs, benches, lamps, and fixtures clean and free from dust?				
Are posters and printed materials clean and neatly racked or posted?				
Does the customer's first view of your establishment convey the image of cleanliness and freshness?				

Reprinted by permission of the National Restaurant Association

Form 4.15

GENERAL CLEANLINESS OF DINING AREA

Date Inspected:_____   Inspected by:_____

Item	Y	N	Comments on Deficiencies and Action Required	Date Corrected
Is the floor dirty or littered, particularly with food particles and napkins?				
Are there crumbs or spilled liquid on chairs or benches?				
Are menus food-marked or worn and dirty, and are condiment containers unclean?				
Are table linens food marked? Are they tattered or torn?				
Is tableware cracked, chipped, streaked, or food-soiled or silverware thumb-marked or food-soiled?				
Are insect sprays being used when food is exposed or customers are present?				
Is floor being swept while food is exposed, being served, or when customers are eating?				
Is adequate lighting available for cleaning?				

Reprinted by permission of the National Restaurant Association

Company Standards

Form 4.16

DINING ROOM AND SERVING AREA

Date Inspected: _____   **Inspected by:** _____

Item	Y	N	Comments on Deficiencies and Action Required	Date Corrected
Is dining area, including floor, tables, and chairs, clean and dry?				
Is tableware clean and sanitized and stored in a manner to prevent splash and contamination?				
Are single-service items sorted and dispensed in a sanitary manner?				
Are single-service items disposed of after single use?				
Are clean, sanitary cloths used for wiping down tabletops and used for no other purpose? Are they stored in sanitizing solution between use?				
Are silverware and serving utensils stored and presented in a manner to prevent contamination and to ensure their being picked up by the handles?				
Are cloths or sponges used for wiping water spills on tableware being served to customers clean and dry and used for no other purpose?				

Reprinted by permission of the National Restaurant Association

Form 4.17

RESTROOMS

Date Inspected: _____   **Inspected by:** _____

Item	Y	N	Comments on Deficiencies and Action Required	Date Corrected
Are customer restrooms clean, dry, light, well ventilated, and free of odor?				
Is all sanitary equipment operating satisfactorily?				
Is there a satisfactory supply of soap, tissue, towels, or a hand drying device?				
Are waste containers covered, kept clean, and emptied frequently?				
Is there adequate hot and cold water, tempered by means of a mixing valve or combination faucet?				
Is there any sign of rodents or insects?				
Are toilet doors solid, self-closing, and in good working order?				

Reprinted by permission of the National Restaurant Association

Company Standards

Form 4.18

SENSORY FACTORS

Date Inspected: _____   **Inspected by:** _____

Item	Y	N	Comments on Deficiencies and Action Required	Date Corrected
Is dining area too hot or cold for customer comfort?				
Is heat and steam from serving line unpleasant for customers (and the servers)?				
Is light in dining area too bright and glary?				
Is light so dim that customers have difficulty seeing the menu, food, and tableware?				
Is clatter of dish and warewashing offensive to customers?				
Is loudness of serving personnel offensive and distracting to customers?				
Is removal of soiled tableware noisy?				
Does odor of the kitchen greet customers as they enter the dining area?				
Is there an "old grease" odor in the dining room, or has it exhausted to the street or parking area?				
Is spoiled food disposed of promptly to prevent obnoxious odor?				

Reprinted by permission of the National Restaurant Association

Form 4.19

WAREWASHING AND STORAGE

Date Inspected:_____   Inspected by:_____

Item	Y	N	Comments on Deficiencies and Action Required	Date Corrected
Are wash and rinse temperatures (proper for the type of machine and ware being washed) being maintained? (See manufacturer's specifications on data plate.)				
Is rinse temperature of at least 170°F being maintained for tableware and utensils? (Manual dishwashing.)				
Are dishes and utensils being scraped and flushed prior to washing?				
Is detergent concentration being maintained at the necessary level for effective washing?				
Is separate personnel used for removing and storing clean tableware, or do warewashing personnel wash hands between handling soiled tableware and sanitized ware?				
Is warewashing equipment cleaned after each day's use to remove chemicals, food particles, soil, and debris?				

Reprinted by permission of the National Restaurant Association

Company Standards

Form 4.19 (continued)

Item	Y	N	Comments on Deficiencies and Action Required	Date Corrected
Are jets and nozzles cleaned of food particles and other obstructions and contaminants?				
Are cleaned and sanitized wares and utensils stored off the floor and in a clean, dry location?				
Is improper toweling of tableware and utensils observed?				

Form 4.20

GARBAGE AND TRASH STORAGE AND DISPOSAL AREAS

Date Inspected:_____   Inspected by:_____

Item	Y	N	Comments on Deficiencies and Action Required	Date Corrected
Is area generally clean, orderly, and free of spilled food and liquids?				
Is floor, platform or ground surface free from spilled particles of food, and constructed of nonabsorbent material such as concrete or asphalt?				
Is area free from objectionable odor?				
Are spilled food particles and litter present in front of incinerator, dumpsters, etc.?				
Are trash and garbage containers clean on the outside?				
If can liners are not in use, are all garbage containers closed with tight-fitting covers?				
Is trash confined in orderly fashion or in suitable containers?				
Is there accumulation of trash or garbage because of infrequent pick-up?				
Are there puddles of wash water and food particles and liquids?				

Reprinted by permission of the National Restaurant Association

Company Standards

Form 4.20 (continued)

Item	Y	N	Comments on Deficiencies and Action Required	Date Corrected
Is there any evidence of rats, ratholes, or nests in the vicinity of the disposal area?				
Are empty garbage and refuse containers washed prior to being returned to use?				
Is mop water properly disposed of as sewage?				
Are drain plugs in place on those containers designed with drains?				
Are hot water, brushes, and detergent or steam provided for washing containers?				
Is room constructed of easily cleanable non-absorbent material?				

Form 4.21

STORAGE ROOMS FOR SUPPLIES AND EQUIPMENT

Date Inspected:_____   Inspected by:_____

Item	Y	N	Comments on Deficiencies and Action Required	Date Corrected
Are storage facilities for supplies and equipment clean, dry, and free of trash and debris?				
Are storage facilities free of empty cartons and wrappings that might provide nesting for rodents?				
Are supplies stored in a neat and orderly manner?				
Are supplies stored off the floor and away from walls to permit access for cleaning and to prevent harborage of rodents and roaches?				
Is perishable or unpackaged food present?				
Are containers of pesticides in a marked cabinet and apart from detergents and other chemicals?				
Is there evidence of rodents or insects?				
Are single-service articles stored at least 6" off the floor in closed containers and not placed under exposed sewer or water lines?				
Are utensils, single service items, or food equipment stored in toilet rooms?				

Reprinted by permission of the National Restaurant Association

Company Standards

Form 4.22

EMPLOYEE FACILITIES (Toilets, lavatories, locker rooms, lunchrooms)

Date Inspected:_____ Inspected by:_____

Item	Y	N	Comments on Deficiencies and Action Required	Date Corrected
Are employees' facilities clean, dry, and free from odor?				
Is there sufficient soap, towels, and tissue for employee needs?				
Is all sanitary equipment operational and in good repair?				
Are proper receptacles available for waste materials?				
Are these receptacles emptied frequently?				
Are soiled uniforms and other soiled clothing improperly stored in lockers or left in the facilities?				
Are containers provided for soiled employees' uniforms?				
Is unwrapped food stored in lockers or left in employee facilities?				
Is there evidence of rodents or insects in the facilities?				

Reprinted by permission of the National Restaurant Association

Form 4.23

MECHANICAL ROOMS

Date Inspected:_____   Inspected by:_____

Item	Y	N	Comments on Deficiencies and Action Required	Date Corrected
Are boiler rooms, compressor rooms, and other utilities rooms clean, dry, and free of foods, soiled or greasy utensils, and food preparation equipment?				
Are they free of soiled linen and rags, empty containers and cartons, trash and debris?				
Is there evidence of rodents and insects?				
Is adequate ventilation provided?				

Reprinted by permission of the National Restaurant Association

Company Standards

Form 4.24

BUILDING

Date Inspected: _____   **Inspected by:** _____

Item	Y	N	Comments on Deficiencies and Action Required	Date Corrected
Are all exits unobstructed and well lit?				
Do all exit doors open easily?				
Are exit lights operating and exit signs visible?				
Do standby emergency lights operate properly?				
Are fire doors operating properly?				
Are fire escapes clear of obstruction?				
Are "No Smoking" signs displayed where appropriate?				
Is the number of occupants held within the listed capacities?				
Are decorations made of flameproof or noncombustible materials?				
Are bottled gas cylinders (outside of building) properly supported and protected from physical damage?				

Reprinted by permission of the National Restaurant Association

Form 4.25

ELECTRICAL

Date Inspected:_____   Inspected by:_____

Item	Y	N	Comments on Deficiencies and Action Required	Date Corrected
Are your premises free from defective wiring or equipment?				
Are flexible cords prohibited from use as a subsitute for fixed wiring?				
Are covers of fuse and switch boxes kept closed?				
Are fuses on lighting and small appliance circuits of proper capacity?				
Are main entrance switches and panel boards unobstructed and readily accessible?				
Are circuits on panel boards properly identified?				
Are plugs on all appliances kept tight and properly grounded?				
Is there adequate clearance around electrical equipment to prevent motors from overheating?				

Reprinted by permission of the National Restaurant Association

Company Standards

Form 4.26

FIRE PROTECTION

Date Inspected:_____   **Inspected by:**_____

Item	Y	N	Comments on Deficiencies and Action Required	Date Corrected
Are all fire extinguishers properly mounted, easy to see, and easy to get to?				
Are all fire extinguishers identified for use? (Class of fire?)				
Are all fire extinguishers tagged, noting monthly inspection and annual maintenance?				
Are extinguishers of proper size and type for protection from hazard?				
Have the automatic sprinkler systems, standpipe, and hose installations been inspected within the past year and are they in operable condition?				
If cooking equipment has been added or relocated, have appropriate changes been made in the extinguisher system?				

Reprinted by permission of the National Restaurant Association

Form 4.27

HEATING AND AIR CONDITIONING EQUIPMENT

Date Inspected:_____   Inspected by:_____

Item	Y	N	Comments on Deficiencies and Action Required	Date Corrected
Is heating furnace checked at regular intervals?				
Are filters cleaned or changed regularly?				
Is all heating equipment, including chimney, gas appliances, flues, smokepipes, and air ducts in good condition and well maintained?				
Are motors properly maintained and clean?				
Are all fan louvers clean?				
Have fans been checked for defective wiring?				
Is the proper type and size of fire extinguisher located in close proximity to HVAC equipment?				

Reprinted by permission of the National Restaurant Association

Company Standards

Form 4.28

HOUSEKEEPING

Date Inspected:_____   **Inspected by:**_____

Item	Y	N	Comments on Deficiencies and Action Required	Date Corrected
Are all accumulations of refuse or rubbish removed from the premises?				
Is combustible material stored away from heating equipment?				
Is the attic space clean?				
Are all boxes stored at least 18 inches below sprinkler heads?				
Are combustible materials properly stored and identified?				
Are employee lockers cleaned and inspected regularly?				

Reprinted by permission of the National Restaurant Association

Form 4.29

KITCHEN

Date Inspected:_____   Inspected by:_____

Item	Y	N	Comments on Deficiencies and Action Required	Date Corrected
Are cooking appliances installed away from combustible materials?				
Is the hood and duct free of grease accumulation?				
Are the filters cleaned at regular intervals?				
Has the automatic fire protection system been inspected and serviced by qualified persons in the last six months?				
Are nonflammable solvents or cleaning aids used for hoods, fans, ducts, and removal devices?				
Have thermostats on cooking equipment been inspected by authorized maintenance contractor?				
Are air quality control devices maintained and cleaned as required?				
Are portable fire extinguishers adjacent to the cooking equipment of the "20BC" rating?				
Are other fire extinguishers in the kitchen of the approved type and in proper number?				

Reprinted by permission of the National Restaurant Association

Company Standards

Form 4.29 (continued)

Item	Y	N	Comments on Deficiencies and Action Required	Date Corrected
Are areas adjoining cooking equipment free of food or rubbish accumulation?				
Is grease buildup prevented by frequent and thorough cleaning of kitchen equipment and surfaces?				

Form 4.30

PERSONNEL

Date Inspected:_____   **Inspected by:**_____

Item	Y	N	Comments on Deficiencies and Action Required	Date Corrected
Have employees been trained to use fire extinguishers?				
Do employees know the location of fire extinguishers?				
Are the telephone numbers of the fire department and other emergency services readily accessible?				
Have employees been instructed in evacuation procedures for both guests and employees? Have they been trained not to show undue alarm and to avoid panic?				
Have employees been trained in a "double check" system to be sure all cooking and warming equipment is turned off when preparing to close?				
Do you hold periodic fire drills for your employees, and do they know what to do in case of a fire emergency?				
Have employees been trained to use hand hose lines?				

Reprinted by permission of the National Restaurant Association

Company Standards

Form 4.31

JOB SPECIFICATION WORKSHEET

Job Title: _____

Hours of Work: _____

	Basic **1**	**Competent** **2**	**Leads/ Trains** **3**	**Solves Problems/ Creates** **4**

Personal Requirements: ____

    Age _____

    Appearance _____

    Strength _____

    Endurance _____

    Neatness _____

    Health and Hygiene _____

Posture: ____

    Standing _____

    Walking _____

    Sitting _____

    Stooping _____

    Reaching _____

    Climbing _____

    Lifting _____

    Other _____

Skills: ____

    Accuracy _____

    Acuteness of Senses _____

    Dexterity _____

    Precision _____

    Speed _____

    Verbal _____

    Versatility _____

Form 4.31 (continued)

	Basic 1	Competent 2	Leads/ Trains 3	Solves Problems/ Creates 4
Mental: ____				
Education _____				
Job Knowledge				
Equipment and Tools _____				
Food and Beverage _____				
Service _____				
Sanitation _____				
Judgment, Logic _____				
Planning, Initiative _____				
Characteristics: ____				
Extrovert / Introvert _____				
Aggressive / Submissive _____				
Team Worker/ Independent / Leader _____				
Social Graces _____				
Emotional Stability _____				
Attentive to Detail _____				
Creative _____				
Articulate _____				

Form 4.32

JOB SPECIFICATION WORKSHEET

		Basic 1	Competent 2	Leads/ Trains 3	Solves Problems/ Creates 4
Job Title:	Host / Hostess				
Hours of Work:					

Job Title: _Host / Hostess_

Hours of Work: _____

	Basic 1	Competent 2	Leads/ Trains 3	Solves Problems/ Creates 4
Personal Requirements: 10%				
Age		2		
Appearance			3	
Strength		2		
Endurance		2		
Neatness		2		
Health and Hygiene			3	

Possible: 24 *Total:* 14 *Ratio:* .583

	Basic 1	Competent 2	Leads/ Trains 3	Solves Problems/ Creates 4
Posture: 10%				
Standing		2		
Walking			3	
Sitting	1			
Stooping	1			
Reaching	1			
Climbing	1			
Lifting	1			
Other	1			

Possible: 32 *Total:* 11 *Ratio:* .344

	Basic 1	Competent 2	Leads/ Trains 3	Solves Problems/ Creates 4
Skills: 30%				
Accuracy			3	
Acuteness of Senses		2		
Dexterity		2		
Precision			3	
Speed		2		
Verbal				4
Versatility		2		

Possible: 28 *Total:* 18 *Ratio:* .643

Form 4.32 (continued)

	Basic 1	Competent 2	Leads/ Trains 3	Solves Problems/ Creates 4
Mental: *25%*				
Education		2		
Job Knowledge				
Equipment and Tools			3	
Food and Beverage			3	
Service				4
Sanitation			3	
Judgment, Logic		2		
Planning, Initiative		2		
Possible: 28 *Total:* 19 *Ratio:* .678				
Characteristics: *25%*				
Extrovert / Introvert		2		
Aggressive / Submissive		2		
Team Worker/ Independent / Leader		2		
Social Graces				4
Emotional Stability		2		
Attentive to Detail		2		
Creative				4
Articulate				4
Possible: 32 *Total:* 22 *Ratio:* .687				

   .583 X 10 = 5.83
   .344 X 10 = 3.44
   .643 X 30 = 19.29
   .678 X 25 = 16.95
   .687 X 25 = 17.17
   TOTAL   62.68

Host / Hostess Job Point Value: 62.68

Company Standards

Form 4.33

JOB SPECIFICATION WORKSHEET

	Basic 1	Competent 2	Leads/ Trains 3	Solves Problems/ Creates 4
Job Title: *Dishwasher*				
Hours of Work:				

Personal Requirements: *10%*

	Basic 1	Competent 2	Leads/Trains 3	Solves Problems/Creates 4
Age	1			
Appearance	1			
Strength		2		
Endurance		2		
Neatness		2		
Health and Hygiene		2		

Possible: 24 *Total:* 10 *Ratio:* .416

Posture: *10%*

	Basic 1	Competent 2	Leads/Trains 3	Solves Problems/Creates 4
Standing		2		
Walking		2		
Sitting	1			
Stooping		2		
Reaching		2		
Climbing		2		
Lifting		2		
Other	1			

Possible: 32 *Total:* 14 *Ratio:* .437

Skills: *30%*

	Basic 1	Competent 2	Leads/Trains 3	Solves Problems/Creates 4
Accuracy		2		
Acuteness of Senses	1			
Dexterity		2		
Precision	1			
Speed		2		
Verbal	1			
Versatility		2		

Possible: 28 *Total:* 11 *Ratio:* .393

Form 4.33 (continued)

	Basic 1	Competent 2	Leads/ Trains 3	Solves Problems/ Creates 4
Mental: _25%_				
Education	1			
Job Knowledge				
Equipment and Tools		2		
Food and Beverage		2		
Service	1			
Sanitation		2		
Judgment, Logic		2		
Planning, Initiative	1			

Possible: 28 Total: 10 Ratio: .357

Characteristics: _25%_

Extrovert / Introvert	1			
Aggressive / Submissive	1			
Team Worker/ Independent / Leader		2		
Social Graces	1			
Emotional Stability	1			
Attentive to Detail		2		
Creative	1			
Articulate	1			

Possible: 32 Total: 10 Ratio: .312

   .416 X 10 = 4.16
   .437 X 10 = 4.37
   .393 X 30 = 11.79
   .357 X 25 = 8.92
   .312 X 25 = _7.8_
   TOTAL   37.04

Dish Washer Job Point Value: 37.04

Form 4.34

EVALUATION FORM

DUTIES	POINT VALUE	PERFORMANCE LEVEL	OVERALL EVALUATION
1. Stocks station	4		
2. Sets table	5		
3. Greets guests	9		
4. Takes order	8		
5. Explains menu	9		
6. Picks up order	6		
7. Serves meal	8		
8. Recommends and serves wine	9		
9. Totals and presents check	8		
10. Performs side duties	4		
11. Operates equipment	4		
12. Meets grooming standards	8		
13. Observes sanitation	8		
14. Provides good customer relations	<u>10</u>		
Total	100	300 possible	

Superior	3	300	Outstanding, Highest Reward
Competent	2	250–300	Superior, Middle Reward
Minimum	1	200–300	Competent, Minimum Reward
Below	0		

Chapter 5

Training Employees

ORIENTATION

The purpose of orientation is to create a positive response to the business and the job. If you can create a favorable image, reduce tension and anxiety, and create a positive impact on a new employee, she will be more likely to stay through the critical first days of employment. Training will be easier and the inclination to listen to disgruntled employees afflicted with old timers disease will be lessened.

Orientation should be treated as a way of filling the employee's need to know. What does a brand new employee need to know to start working in your establishment? The checklist on Checklist 5.1 is to ensure that you tell the employee everything and do not forget one or two critical items. It is best to give this information to employees during a one-on-one session. Display the attitude this individual is worthy of your concern, time, and attention and will become a member of your work team.

Theft orientation is a phrase we have borrowed from Robert Martin, the astute and experienced instructor for hotel housekeeping. His ideas on the containment of stealing are valid for food service operations. During initial training and orientation, Martin stresses new employees should be informed of the theft prevention procedures of the company. Such things as random locker inspections and reports to police of missing items should be explained. Posting significant inventory losses for everyone to see and keeping records of missing items for clues to a pattern tells a new employee management will exercise reasonable controls and be diligent in

Checklist 5.1

EMPLOYEE / ORIENTATION CHECKLIST

Name: _____

Job Title: _____

W-4 Form	_____
I-9 Form	_____
Health Care Plan	_____
Name Tag	_____
Employee Handbook	_____

COMPANY INFORMATION

Working Hours and Days	_____	Answering the Telephone	_____
Time Clock	_____	Employee Use of Telephone	_____
Breaks and Meals	_____	Employee Smoking	_____
Days Off		Work Station	_____
Holidays	_____	Supervisor	_____
Sick Days	_____	Department Meetings	_____
Vacation	_____	Uniforms	_____
Unpaid Leave	_____	Grooming Code	_____
Pay Rate	_____	Emergency Procedures	_____
Overtime	_____	Theft Orientation	_____
Pay Day	_____	Tour of Facilities	_____
Employee Parking	_____	Introduction to Other Workers	_____
Entry and Exit to Building	_____	Information About Owner or President of Company (Big Boss)	_____
Restrooms	_____		
Employee Lockers	_____		

trying to prevent theft. This sends a signal that management will help the honest employee protect and maintain her integrity.

All the information on the Orientation Checklist is a great deal of information for one person to absorb in just one session. Be prepared to repeat the needed information several times. The employee handbook will contain basic information, but do not expect the employee to read it until he wants specific information. Tell him the first day in a one-on-one personal session and repeat it during an initial training period whenever a breakdown of communications appears.

JOB TRAINING

On-The-Job-Training

Training always involves two factors: 1) demonstrating the task and telling the trainee how to do it; and 2) watching the trainee perform a task and correcting mistakes. A common method of training is on-the-job-training. The benefit of this method is the new employee is able to use what has been taught immediately. On-the-job-training works best when the person being trained observes a task and then immediately performs the task under the watchful eye of the trainer.

Show and tell is the best method for demonstrating the task: this is how to do it, this is why it is done, and this is what to do for each step as it is performed by the trainer. Do not confuse the trainee with more information than he needs. Keep the language simple and stress the core of the action. Do not rush demonstrating the task. Be sure it is shown correctly as this sets the standard of performance in the trainee's mind.

Have the worker immediately perform the task as she was shown. This is the heart of the learning experience. When she is able to do it right, she has a feeling of achievement that reinforces the learning. The first time performing the task should be considered a trial. Any errors or omissions should be corrected in a positive way. Show the task again if necessary. Have the new worker perform the task and tell you the key points and why they are done the way they are. Continue this routine until you are satisfied she will do it exactly as shown.

Plan the on-the-job-training so the new worker can begin to contribute to the operation from the first day. When you look at all the job units that make up the job, you will see job units that are routine and repeated frequently during one work day. The new person will be able to go through the sequence of observation and supervised performance several times during the day's work. You may then expect a new person to learn the simple units with few tasks in one day's time. Such things as correctly setting each place on the table, preparing appropriate and attractive garnish, making individual pots of coffee, or correctly chopping lettuce for a garden salad are repetitive tasks and with good instruction should be learned quickly.

Other job units, such as setting up a word station or closing a work area, are performed only once during the work day. For the trainee to have an opportunity to practice a once-a-day job, training time prior to the beginning of the shift or after the shift is over must be arranged. If additional training time is not given, it will take several days for the new person to understand and be able to adequately perform without close supervision. The more complex job units, such as taking the food order for a table or preparing the soup du jour will require a longer learning time before the new person can meet the necessary production standards. You may want the person to perform some of the simpler tasks of a complex job unit as a way to quickly begin contributing to the work day. For those job units that do not easily permit observation and practice, you may wish to set up supplemental training to the on-the-job instruction. Written materials may be provided for outside study or a training videotape can be made available.

Who Should Do the Training. On-the-job-training requires careful planning to see the skill training and knowledge needs of the new employee are being met. The selection of the person or persons to do the training is critical. It is always better if the new worker's supervisor can do the training. If this is not practical, then another worker who performs that job will be the training instructor. Be sure the employee instructor wants to do the training, knows how to train, and is given proper recognition.

You want every employee of your operation to have a certain attitude about things like quality, customer relations, and sanitation. It is important the person doing the training imparts the right feeling to the new employee. The desire to train and knowledge of the job are characteristics needed by a training instructor.

Job Experience

When you hire an experienced worker, you must find out how much he already knows and what skills he already has. You do not want to waste time teaching what is already known. Training new workers who have experience should begin with skills tests for the units of work in your operation. Some of the units of work may actually require performing that unit: setting up a work station, serving beverages, making a salad, or broiling a steak medium rare. For some of the units of work or critical activities, a paper and pencil test may be appropriate. Case study problems are often appropriate to get a feel for the attitudes of new workers.

After observing the new worker's performance and analyzing his answers, set up a plan to train what the person does not know or does not perform up to your standard. You want experienced workers to meet the same standards as those people who have worked only for you. Checklist 5.2 illustrates the steps for training an experienced worker. We will go through the process with you using the training plan that was developed for Carol.

Carol is a new server who has been hired to replace Andy. She will work Tuesday through Saturday and must be trained well enough to start work next Tuesday. She has several years experience as a server. Andy's last day will be this Saturday. Carol will come in Thursday at 9:00 a.m. for a pretest. Use the job description (page xxx) to guide the testing procedures for her skills. The test reveals:

1. She stocks the service station in 15 minutes.
2. She sets the tables in less than 3 minutes.
3. She understands most menu items.
4. She does not know your guest check procedure.
5. She prices and totals checks accurately.
6. She does not know your plate preparation procedure.
7. She knows tray service well.

Checklist 5.2

STEPS FOR TRAINING AN EXPERIENCED WORKER

1.	LOOK AT THE JOB	Use the job description to see all the skills, knowledge, and attitudes needed to meet your standard.
2.	ANALYZE PREVIOUS EXPERIENCE	Perform a pretest to find two things: skills, knowledge, and attitudes that meet your standard; and all the items that **do not** meet your standards.
3.	DECIDE TRAINING NEEDS	Subtract what the worker does know and can do from what the worker needs to know and do.
4.	SET UP TRAINING PLAN	Train what the worker does not know and cannot do.
5.	EVALUATE	Follow up and make any improvements needed.

8. She is not familiar with bottle wine service.

9. She responds correctly to all sanitation questions.

10. She is familiar with all equipment except those relating to the service of bottles of wine.

11. She meets grooming requirements.

12. She responds correctly to questions about guest relations.

13. She is not familiar with your wine list.

14. She is familiar with your dessert items.

15. She knows most of your appetizers and some of your specialty items.

Decide Training Needs. After analyzing the pretest results Carol will need training on the following: where to find everything for the service station, the menu items she does not know, guest check procedures, plate preparation procedures, bottle wines and the correct service of them.

Set Up Training Plan. The best time to train Carol is Monday as this is a slow day. Pat is the best person to train Carol for the lunch shift and Jerry is the best person to train for the evening shift. Take an hour Friday to explain the Job Instruction Training method to these two serving people. Give Pat and Jerry the results of the pretest so they will be prepared to train in the areas where Carol needs the most training.

Evaluation. Check regularly Monday to see how things are going. Check again Tuesday as Carol begins to work on her own. If everything is okay, recognize the good work of Carol, Pat, and Jerry in the training process. If there are problems, be supportive and try to mutually solve the problem. Answer any questions any of the three people may have. Check on a regular basis throughout Carol's first week just to reassure and provide support. If this training turns out well, consider giving Pat and Jerry additional training on how to be trainers and additional training assignments.

Training Content

The training content is derived from the procedures sheets that were written during the job breakdown process. All the procedure sheets listed on the job description provide the content for the training for that particular job. We explained these procedure sheets were the basis for our pretest of experienced workers. Carol was the example and represents a typical new worker. Match Carol's training needs with the written and visual guidelines available.

Training Employees 5-7

CAROL—Training Needs

Service station set up	....	Service Station Procedure Sheet
Menu item knowledge	....	Menu
		Recipes
		Menu Policy Guide
		Menu Meetings
		Posted Specials
Guest check procedures	....	Guest Check Procedures Sheet
		Check Payment Procedures Sheet
Plate preparation	....	Plate Preparation Procedures Sheet
Bottle wines	....	Food/Wine Sheet
Service of bottled wine	....	Wine Service Sheet

For example, Carol does not understand all of your menu items. Make available to her the recipes for the menu items she does not understand. During the regular menu meetings with serving staff, encourage Carol (all new people) to ask questions about any item she does not understand. The menu policy guide will explain the allowable substitutions for your menu as well as the substitutions that are not allowable. Your system of posting specials in the kitchen will be explained during her training period.

The Guest Check Procedure Sheet provides the content for training Carol on your method of writing up the guest's order. The Wine Service Procedures Sheet provides the content for training Carol on taking a wine order. Examine the Guest Check Procedure explained on the Standard Procedure Sheet (Form 5.1) and the Wine Service Procedure (Form 5.2). You will see all the details needed to properly train Carol (or any new server) are listed in job sequence order.

Keep all the procedure sheets that go with each job description in a procedures manual for that particular job.

Retraining

Even though people are properly trained for a job, it does not take care of all training needs. Several situations may arise in which further training is necessary. When changes are made that affect the job, further training may be needed. A change may be made on the menu, a new piece of equipment may be installed in the kitchen, or you may decide to use a different linen supplier. It is important to keep your people's knowledge and skills up to date. They cannot do the job well (and feel badly) if the job has changed and no one has thought to tell them about how the change affects their jobs.

Form 5.3, Training Schedule, may be used to inform everyone involved of their training responsibilities. Use the form to suit your own time schedule. It may cover a one-week schedule or even a month. Just be careful not to make it too cluttered. Try to make a ritual of retraining by posting a new training schedule at least once a month.

Another useful form for implementing training is a Professional Growth Plan (Form 5.4). This form can serve as a contract for you to provide training and for the employee to master the training. This contract is not necessary for all training that takes place within your operation but it is important to put into writing what is expected of both parties when professional growth is the goal. For example, you and Mary have decided she is ready to move into a position with more responsibility. The skills she must master are listed on the job description for a host/hostess. The qualifications she must demonstrate are listed on the Job Specification. You both agree on the skills she will learn and a reasonable time frame for mastery of these skills. As one plan is accomplished, another is implemented. This gives you checkpoints for her progress and allows you to plan for when she will begin the new position. She will be able to work to achieve her goal and will be able to assume the responsibility for her professional growth. If you are planning to expand, just think about the value of a system that gives your employees a chance to grow.

We should also mention the kind of training needed when an employee's performance drops below par. You cannot tolerate poor performance. The employee's respect for you will be reduced, the job will be degraded, and the individual will develop a poor self-image. Often this situation calls for an approach generally referred to as counseling and coaching. Coaching and counseling is the subject of material in Chapter 7.

We will talk about the mechanics of setting up a system for training in Chapter 7. Retraining current employees needs to be a part of your on-going training system. Retraining may be necessary when changes are made, when employee performance is not up to standard, or when employees request more training for continued growth on the job.

COOPERATIVE OR APPRENTICE

We have known the value of the questioning process since old Socrates gathered his students about him. When you train an apprentice or a cooperative education student, the questioning method will be an important part of the learning process.

The cooperative method or an apprenticeship implies the help of another institution in the development of a trained worker. This other institution will require the student worker to provide regular progress reports. This reporting process will take the form of questions testing the employee's job knowledge. By cooperating with the worker's institutional supervisor, you may take advantage of this process and stress the methods and standards you have set for your operation. This process will reinforce your training program.

The apprentice or the cooperative education student will have a set of competencies she is expected to master on the job or in the classroom. You want to plan to have the employee master the skills in your operation that you wish to control. Each institution may have its own set of competencies but they all fall into the following categories of work sequences that were listed on the Job Analysis Worksheet: set up a work station, obtain needed materials and supplies, produce food or beverage item, produce clean utensils or equipment, prepare product for service, communicate with customer, serve food or beverage item to customer, handle money, provide information for reports, provide input for menu development, and participate in promotional activities. The following critical activities that are listed on the Job Analysis Worksheet are also needed competencies: recognize and maintain quality standards, follow sanitary procedures, maintain good customer relations, meet dress and grooming standards, demonstrate creativity, and personalize work.

Form 5.5 is an example of a learning contract you may prepare for the apprenticing employee. When the apprenticing employee is brought into your operation, think about what you need from a productive employee in that job position. Talk to the cooperative or apprentice teacher and find out the new employee's level of skill. Have the apprentice or co-op student sign the contract to learn the skills that you need and will teach as part of your own training plan. The cooperative teacher or apprentice supervisor will sign the contract and also assist in supervising the learning experiences of the student. The procedures and methods the apprenticing employees learn from your training will be reinforced in classroom training sessions. The classroom training teacher will have more time to expand on the theory of work-related skills. This will provide you with an employee with a good foundation for growth and mastery of food service occupations. The rating system on the learning contract provides a method for you to give input into the student grade.

We have listed the state offices that supervise cooperative education in Appendix A. These offices will be able to provide you with the names of teachers and schools in your community involved in supervising cooperative education students.

We have also listed the local chapters of the American Culinary Federation and a contact person for apprenticeship training. You may contact the nearest local chapter for information on hiring and working with apprentices. You will find this list in Appendix B.

PRINCIPLES FOR THE TRAINEE

Start the day right by arriving at the job before the scheduled workday begins. Allow yourself time to gather your thoughts and prepare yourself for the day's training activities. Chefs use the term **mise in place**, which means roughly that everything that is needed to perform a particular job is there and ready to go (Walk and Pike, 1989). Mise in place can apply to the beginning of a training workday. The required reading of policies and procedures should be accomplished and any questions raised in your mind should be written down. View the training as an opportunity to learn the right way to do things and maintain an open and accepting attitude. Try to use any past experience as a connection to learning the way things are done in this operation and do not even hint that it was a better way.

It is essential that you understand what is expected of you so the more questions you ask up front the better. You need to know what your boss wants you to do. Feel free to ask questions so you understand what you are doing. Be patient with yourself and with the person answering your questions; in time you will understand production schedules or any other written materials that guide the day's work. Find out where the restaurant keeps procedures books or other reference material that can help you understand what is expected of you and ask when this material is accessible to employees.

On a new job you may want to keep a notepad handy to write down how to do things as they are explained to you. This makes it easier to follow the right steps the next time you have to do the same thing. If the training sessions do not allow for you to write things down as they are explained, you can do it later when time permits.

A sensitive area for a new employee is how to get along with the other workers. A good rule is to be courteous. Also, always be neat and clean up after yourself. Be careful about getting involved in politics at the workplace. Be your own person. Make up your own mind. Avoid small talk except during breaks. Remember, the person who tries to get attention by talking about personal difficulties and troubles quickly turns people off. As a new worker, keep your private life at home.

In most any work environment, a positive and patient attitude will allow you the time to learn to perform your duties efficiently and effectively. To sum up:

Arrive on time.

Learn how to do the tasks assigned to you.

Ask questions about your job.

Pay attention to detail.

Be courteous to fellow employees.

Practice positive thinking.

Be pleasant.

Be patient.
(Walk and Pike, 1989)

INSTRUCTOR PRINCIPLES

There are skills needed to successfully train others. Learn how to prepare for training and learn all you can about how people learn. In Chapter 6, we will discuss how to set up a training plan and how adults learn. Try to understand how the trainee feels. Make the connections from the trainee's life experiences to the value of learning the task at hand. Lead the trainee to want to learn by your own enthusiasm and belief in performance standards. Remember you are teaching more than skills and procedures. You are giving an example of your own work ethic and many subtle lessons in human relations.

Most new employees are anxious about the job. Anxiety and fear will reduce our ability to learn. A wise trainer puts the new employee at ease, recognizes small successes, and tries to establish a relationship of trust.

Sometimes when you know a job so well it is second nature to you, it is hard to set a pace that is appropriate for the new person. Be patient and sensitive to the person you are teaching. People learn best when the training enhances their self-image. Recognize the individual's learning rate and recognize what the person already knows. If you teach too fast or too slow the person will lose interest and not pay attention. Do not just teach tasks, teach people.

Keep the instruction real. You may teach a general principle, but it must be applied to a specific situation. People learn best by hands-on experience. You can read a book about how to open a wine bottle, but the skill is learned by opening a bottle of wine. Use words they can understand: simple words, familiar words, and words that help them understand.

Training should be planned with each session carefully outlined. Think through exactly what should be learned and how it will be taught. People generally learn better when they see the whole picture and then learn the specific tasks. Show a complete unit of work and then break it down to the tasks needed to complete that unit of work. Let the trainee start with the basic tasks and then progress to the more complex tasks.

Have all materials on-hand for each training session. See that all equipment works. Have a place that is free of interruptions and allows concentration. Check the environmental factors. A place that is poorly ventilated or too hot can rapidly put people to sleep.

Whether the task is simple or complex, pleasant or unpleasant, always keep a positive attitude. You do not want to imply a negative attitude to either the task or the new employee.

When a mistake is made, correct the action rather than the person, and correct by helping, not by criticizing. A useful technique is to complement before correcting. Say, for example, "You are holding the bottle exactly right and you have poured exactly the right amount of wine. What you need to do to avoid spilling is to raise the mouth and turn the bottle slightly before you draw it away from the glass." (Instead of, "Look what you did. You dribbled wine all over the table. Don't do that. I told you to raise the mouth!") Emphasize what is right, not what is wrong (Miller and Porter, 1985).

To sum up:
Teach people.
Set a good example.
Establish a relationship of trust.
Be sensitive to the level of the learner.
Keep it simple, concrete, practical, and real.
Organize the training session.
Praise each success.
Be positive.
Correct the action, do not criticize the learner.
Be patient.

Career Ladder

When you wrote the job list, you noted that some jobs were entry-level positions. As you perform the job analysis, you can see that some tasks require a higher level of skill. What you want is a hierarchy of skill mastery from the least to the greatest. A person may come to you without skill and move in a normal pattern to a higher level of mastery of skills. We usually group

Training Employees

5-13

together skills of an equal level into a job title. The person moving into greater mastery of skills will move from one job to the next job of a higher skill level. When you write down this progression from one job to the next you have structured a career ladder for your operation.

In food service operation, the career ladder has the following two sides: back of the house and front of the house. Form 5.6 is a simplified version of a career ladder for a food service operation. The career ladder for your own operation will resemble this structure. Some levels may have several positions that can be used as a stepping stone to the next level. For example, you may have many different cooks that with further training could develop supervisory skills and assume supervisory positions.

Path for the Employee. Most of us like to feel we have control of our lives. The presence of a career ladder shows an employee she can initiate a change to gain more skill and move into a better position. When training and retraining are on-going activities in your operation, every employee will see there is an opportunity to grow. By developing job descriptions and job specifications, you are equipped to guide the path of an employee to personal improvement. For example, the job specification for a host/hostess (Form 3.6) tells you this person must demonstrate leadership ability and be attentive to all the details required for excellent dining room service. When Mary demonstrates an ability to take on more responsibility and expresses a desire to learn more, you guide her path for learning more of the details about providing excellent dining room service. People can learn leadership skills but a short course in supervision is advised.

While the career ladder is a structured progression of skill mastery, the employee's path for career development may need a more individualized approach. Some employees may already possess some of the skills or characteristics needed for the next level. Their path should allow them to begin mastery of the skills they lack. Some employees may want to rotate to another job on the same skill level rather than progress on a career ladder. The Professional Growth Plan form provides a way to give individual attention to the training needs of the employee. If you want to devise a grand master plan for the path an employee should follow, the job specifications and the job descriptions will tell you the steps of the path.

Consider which skills are best taught in your operation and which skills are best learned somewhere else. For example, the host/hostess requires some aggressiveness to insist upon meticulous standards of service. There are excellent workshops and short courses available for assertiveness.

Job skills are best taught within your operation. You want employees to perform according to your standards. Previous experience or education may speed the learning process, but the job skills must be the skills required to serve your customers.

Employee Potential. You have invested a great deal of money for equipment that will depreciate over time. Over time, your employees have the potential to appreciate and increase in value. Training and professional growth will give you a more valuable workforce.

REFERENCES

Forrest, Lewis C., Jr. 1990. *Training for the Hospitality Industry.* East Lansing, MI: Educational Institute of the American Hotel and Motel Association, pp. 64-67, 89-97, 164-167.

Martin, Robert. 1986. *Professional Management of Housekeeping Operations.* New York: John Wiley and Sons, pp. 151-157, 161, 289-302.

Miller, Jack E. and Mary Porter. 1985. *Supervision in the Hospitality Industry.* New York: John Wiley and Sons, pp. 148-150, 157, 163-165.

Walk, Mary and Nancy Pike. 1989. *Guiding Your Internship,* Englewood Cliffs, NJ: Prentice-Hall, pp. 115 and 116.

Form 5.1

STANDARD PROCEDURE SHEET

Job: Waiter / Waitress.　　　**Unit:** Communicates with Customers

Task No. 3: Guest Check Procedure

1. On guest check, number seats at table.

2. Ask each guest in turn what he or she wants and record following the appropriate seat number.

3. Suggest additional items such as appetizer, soup, salad, beverage, wine, specials.

4. Ask for all "choice of" selections and record on check.

5. Use correct abbreviations.

6. Turn in order to kitchen.

7. Complete guest check with prices.

Attachments:

Copy of guest check
Menu abbreviations

Form 5.2

STANDARD PROCEDURE SHEET

Job: Waiter / Waitress. **Unit:** Communicates with Customers

Task No. 2: Take the wine order

1. Know the wine list.

2. Ask, "Have you chosen a wine?"

3. Be prepared to help with selection.

4. If asked to help, ask questions to understand guest preferences: red, white, blush, dry, semi-sweet.

5. Suggest two or three within preferences. Allow guest to make selection.

6. Do not try to intimidate the guest with your knowledge. Always strive to be helpful and courteous.

7. If guests order individual glasses of wine, record selection on appropriate seat number.

8. Excuse yourself from the table.

Training Employees

Form 5.3

TRAINING SCHEDULE

Employee	Linens Tom	Tilting Skillet Hobart	Hostess Tom Maria	Order Food Kathy	Dress / Grooming Film
Average Training Time	**30 Min**	**2 Hours**	**8 Hours**	**4 Hours**	**1 Hour**
1. Mary	9/11		9/10-9/17		9/13 a.m.
2. Keith		9/10		9/12-9/13	
3. Tim	9/11				9/13
4. Rachael	9/11				9/13
5. Doug		9/10			9/13
6. Jean		9/10			9/13

Training Times:
 Tuesday and Wednesday 9:00–10:30 a.m.
 Monday, Wednesday, and Thursday 1:30–3:30 p.m.

Unless you are notified otherwise, training sessions will begin promptly at 9:00 in the morning or 1:30 in the afternoon.

Form 5.4

PROFESSIONAL GROWTH PLAN

Name: _____	Date: _____

Position: _____

Type of Training: _____

Objective: _____

Tasks	Date Achieved—Signature
Study sales history to forecast workloads	_____
Prepare work schedule to meet needs	_____
Perform inspection of dining room and prepare report	_____
Requisition supplies	_____
Receive and store supplies	_____
Understand Job Analysis procedure, Job Description, Job Specification, and Job Breakdown for serving personnel	_____

Submit any suggestions for improvement in writing.

Form 5.5

LEARNING CONTRACT

Name: _____	**Semester:** _____
Training Station: _____	
Supervisor: _____	**Telephone:** _____
Training Position: _____	
Career Goal: _____	

Learning Outcome Goals	Assessment
	Do not know / Poor / Average / Outstanding
1. _____ _____ _____	
2. _____ _____ _____	
3. _____ _____ _____	
4. _____ _____ _____	

Comments

_____
_____
_____

Student
Signature _____

Supervisor
Signature _____

Teacher _____

Form 5.6

ORGANIZATIONAL STRUCTURE

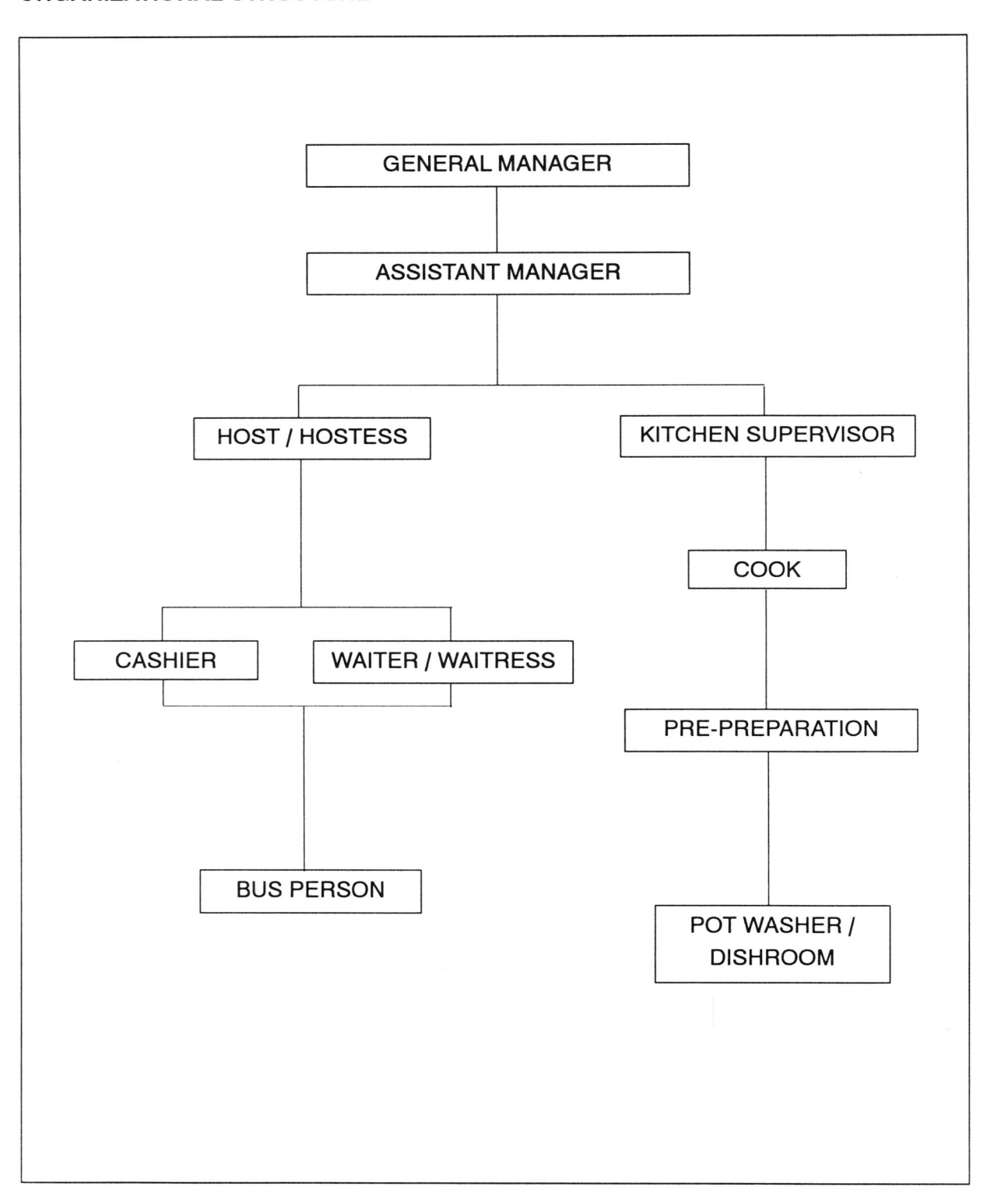

```
                    GENERAL MANAGER
                           |
                   ASSISTANT MANAGER
                           |
              ┌────────────┴────────────┐
        HOST / HOSTESS            KITCHEN SUPERVISOR
              |                          |
              |                         COOK
              |                          |
     ┌────────┴────────┐                 |
  CASHIER      WAITER / WAITRESS         |
              |                   PRE-PREPARATION
              |                          |
         BUS PERSON              POT WASHER /
                                  DISHROOM
```

Chapter 6

Training Fundamentals

CHARACTER OF EMPLOYEES

We have been spoiled by our history as an industry. Early roadside inns and local taverns were family affairs. The husband was the host and innkeeper, the wife did the cooking, and the children did the innkeeping chores with the help of an aunt, uncle, and a servant or two. There was no need for much training because the work was a family effort and everyone knew their jobs. In the nineteenth century, as hotels, taverns, and the new restaurant dining rooms followed the railroad across the country, floods of immigrants from Europe entered our country looking for work. These immigrants had grown up as servants or had served long apprenticeships in restaurant kitchens and knew how to do the work. During the depression, willing workers from other industries entered the restaurant industry and worked hard to learn their jobs because they needed an income to survive.

Today's worker is much more likely to be a short-term or part-time worker who is working in our restaurant until something else comes along. People who do not expect to stay long on a job are not willing to make a commitment and are not interested in learning very much about the job. They want the paycheck at the end of the week and do not think about this job as a long-time career. They are not interested in reading training materials and are bored by lectures. They are impatient and are looking for a skill they can do this afternoon.

Diversity is another characteristic of our workforce—age diversity, cultural diversity, and racial diversity. We have people who do not speak English. We have people who are in college or are college graduates, and we have people with developmental disabilities or physical handicaps. We have bright people, timid people, strong independent people, school dropouts, and professional students. Many have never had a job before; others have been in the industry for a long time. How can you train such different people for the same jobs and expect the same performance standards?

To accomplish this, you need a way of training that trains everyone to your standard. You want a training system that adapts to individual needs and lends itself to one-on-one training. We are going to discuss in detail how to set up a training program that gives immediate skills, sows the seed for continuous growth, and allows you to train people as individuals. We will tell you about training fundamentals and you can apply the ones that work best for your operation.

THE ADULT LEARNING PROCESS

We want to tell you something about how adults learn. Learning is the acquisition of knowledge, skill, or attitudes. Learning may also be defined as a change in behavior due to a life experience. If we want training to cause the desired behavior, we must plan the experience to meet the needs of the adult learner.

1. Adults must want to learn. They must feel a personal desire to master new behavior because it will be of benefit to them.

2. Adults will only learn when they feel the need to learn. They want to know, "How is this going to help me?" Adults learn best when the knowledge or skill will be immediately applied to solve a problem that is presently occurring.

3. Adults learn best by doing. Learning is faster and retention is longer when adults practice using what they are learning.

4. Adults learn best if the training solves real problems. It should be focused on specific, real-world situations.

5. Adult learning must be integrated with past experience. If the new information does not fit with past experience, it will be rejected. New ideas must be reinforced by past experience.

6. Adults appreciate an orderly, but informal, classroom. When trainees are treated as professionals who accept adult responsibilities for their own learning, they will respond with responsible adult behavior. When they are treated as

immature people who must be controlled, they will react immaturely.

7. Learning occurs more quickly when the information reaches the learner through a variety of channels. Demonstrations, audio-visual materials, and participation in the learning process all increase the impact of the training. Behavior is not easy to change in adults and repetition and reinforcement are necessary for learning.

8. Adults need to know they are learning correctly. They need guidance on how well they are doing and whether they are grasping the basic ideas (Forrest, 1990).

JOB INSTRUCTION TRAINING

Successful training observes adult learning needs. During World War II, millions of workers had to be trained quickly to operate the war plants. At that time, a training method was developed that takes maximum advantage of how adults learn. This method is called Job Instruction Training (JIT). It has been used in various forms in all kinds of training programs in all types of industry. The JIT method consists of four basic steps:

1. Prepare workers for training. Explain how this training will benefit them. See that they are ready to receive the training.

2. Demonstrate what the worker is to do (show and tell). Have the worker receive the information by hearing and seeing.

3. Have the worker do the task as shown. Let the worker explain what is being done and why. Repeat until performance is satisfactory. Recognize what is done correctly and correct mistakes in the tasks.

4. Follow through—Put the worker on the job, checking, recognizing good work, and correcting as needed.

In the first step, the learner sees the need for training. This is an important preparation for the training, for without a need, a reason, or a benefit, the person will not learn.

With the second step the person acquires knowledge about what is to be done. He learns about the task (for example, how to deep fry potatoes). He sees how it is done, and hears what is done and why.

At step three, learners are allowed to practice what they are learning. They receive guidance from the trainer and from the performance itself. If the potatoes are overcooked, they know something is wrong. If the potatoes are golden brown, they know what they did is right. They have solved a real problem.

The fourth step is a positive consequence of mastering the task. This provides a feeling of achievement, a sense of success, while reinforcing the learning.

A TRAINING PLAN

As we show you how to write a training plan, keep in mind the JIT method and how adults learn.

The procedure sheets developed as a result of the job breakdown process are the basis for training each individual using a one-on-one method of instruction. We will use the Standard Procedure Sheet for the following two tasks of a waiter/waitress to write a training plan: Explains the Menu and Guest Check Procedures (Form 6.1, 6.2). These two tasks are performed at the same time, even though the wait person must use two different skills. These procedure sheets were written during the job breakdown process. Together, with the standard procedure sheets for all the work units, and all the critical activities for the job of waiter/waitress, these sheets form the procedures manual for that job.

A training plan puts into a logical sequence all the learning activities for each training session. It tells what you will train someone to do, the method to be used for training, how long training will take, what supplies and materials you need, and how you will evaluate what has been learned. Form 6.4 is an example of a training plan for the tasks of the waiter/waitress job, Explains the Menu and Guest Check Procedures.

Let's go through it step-by-step.

Notice that the training objective is written as a performance standard so you can measure whether the training reaches the objective. The tasks are taught in several training sessions. The primary reason for this is to avoid giving the trainee too much to learn at once. One hour and thirty minutes is considered the best time frame for holding the attention of an adult in a learning situation. Two hours is the maximum. Avoid tying up the person doing the training for too long. Teachers also have limitations.

The trainee should be shown the complete sequence of greeting the customer and taking the order. It helps the trainee to see the complete work unit before breaking it down into individual task components. This training plan uses a videotape to show the whole unit. It is possible to have the trainee observe this work unit in the dining room. The whole unit can also be shown as a demonstration in the training room before beginning the role-play and JIT of each component.

Greeting the customer and taking the order requires a foundation of knowledge—knowledge of the menu. Knowledge is best acquired by private study. Ideally, you will have a programmed instruction unit for menu knowledge. If this is not possible, reading recipes and menu policy guidelines and talking to the chef are other methods of acquiring menu knowledge.

After menu knowledge has been acquired, the tasks are taught in the order in which they are performed on the job. One training session may include several components depending on the learning time for each component of the tasks. When writing the training plan, estimate the training time required for an inexperienced worker. This time can than be adjusted according to the individual being trained.

Feedback from the JIT method provides an evaluation of how the worker is progressing toward achievement of the objective. The training objective is more lenient than the performance standard for a fully-trained employee. Remember, adults like to know how they are doing.

Your training materials should include the same equipment and supplies that are used on the job and any special training materials such as videotapes. They should all be available and ready before the training starts. This keeps the training sessions orderly and promotes a professional image. You must prepare your entire session in advance if training time is to be effective and not wasted on irrelevant distractions.

Developing a written training plan helps you to think through all the details of the training and gives you a blueprint for training activities.

In chapter 7, we will discuss establishing a training system. The written training plan is a prior requirement to a system.

Training Results

In reality, there are only two results that will occur after a training program: either the new worker will be able to perform or the new worker will not be able to perform. Let us consider we are training Margie and Tom, who have not worked as wait people before. Carry out your training plan (Form 6.4) training them for every component in the learning activities. Evaluate them at every place for feedback to make sure they are learning what you want them to learn and are meeting your performance standards. When you have taught all the components of the tasks, evaluate Margie and Tom by having them perform the entire sequence of these two tasks.

Margie meets the performance standard and demonstrates an ability to meet training objectives. She will now learn the next unit of the job, Serving Food and Beverages.

Tom has problems and fails to meet the standard for these two tasks. He is retrained in those procedures he is not doing correctly. If he did not answer questions about the menu correctly, have him study some more.

If he keeps having problems, you might try him on the next unit, Serving Food and Beverages, anyway. If he does not learn that either, he may not be able to handle this job, and you may have to place him in a less demanding job, busperson perhaps. This tells you something may be wrong with your selection procedures. Also consider that your training may not have been appropriate and you have to take a look at that.

If you do not have an opening for a busperson, or if he does not learn that job, you may have to let him go. What is important about this story is the training time has not been wasted because it identified an untrainable employee within the probation period. It can be frustrating though.

TRAINING PROBLEMS AND TRAINING BENEFITS

Problems for Training

Let's discuss some of the very real problems that surround training. A very real problem is time. It takes your time to teach and the worker's time to learn. You may often have an urgent need for someone who can do the work right now and you do not have the time to do a good job of training.

Another big problem is cost. Your time and the worker's time costs money. Training cost is often a cost that is neglected when you are making financial plans. Training is an investment in the future and you may need to prove this to your friendly banker.

Frustration is a problem. Our normal response to frustration is to avoid the immediate cause of the frustration. Many times, workers just get trained and then quit. Or, like Tom in our story, they cannot or do not respond to training. It can be easy to give up on training because we simply quit trying. This temporarily reduces our frustration.

The failure to clearly communicate our expectation can cause a problem. Sometimes the task is so routine we fail to communicate exactly what is to be done: for example, how to lift heavy boxes without hurting your back, how to sanitize cutting boards, how to handle knives to avoid getting cut, or how to hand a menu to the customer so the customer reads the star item. They seem so simple to us, we think everybody should know them.

Sometimes we feel the tasks are unpleasant or even degrading. We prejudge the people who will perform this task as somehow lesser people. This feeling toward the person will show in the way we train. Every task is necessary to the successful operation of the restaurant and the person who performs the task is a part of our success.

The complexity of training for a job that requires creative skills or communications skills can be a problem. It can be hard to define all the tasks performed by a creative chef. Equally difficult is helping a person learn the subtle skills of building rapport with a customer.

You can probably add a paragraph or two right here about how hard it is to train. Before everyone gets too discouraged and depressed, let us point out some of the benefits of training.

Training Benefits

Employees like to know exactly what behavior is expected of them. They want to know how to correctly perform the job for which they were hired. Good training gets them through the painful first days on the job and smoothes the initiation into a competent work crew. They do not always have to be asking questions. They do not make so many mistakes that they get negative feedback from bosses or crew members.

Bosses like to use their time effectively. They do not like to get stuck watching and helping one worker struggling to meet production needs. They do not like to fill in for the worker who quits in frustration or spend all their time solving problems created by incompetent workers. They like to manage, not fight fires.

Good training teaches each employee how to perform each job to your standards. Everyone learns how to do the job so the customer receives the same consistent good service and the same consistent good product every visit to the restaurant. Satisfied customers create a positive image for your restaurant.

The employees can feel good about themselves because they know how to do their job. They know they are meeting your standards and they will be a part of a work crew that keeps customers happy. A satisfied employee will have a more positive attitude, will be more productive, and will stay with you longer. This will reduce turnover and you will not have to spend so much time trying to figure out how to motivate a constantly changing work crew.

Employees that know what they are doing will help keep costs down. There will be less breakage, less waste, and less spoilage. Employees with good morale have fewer accidents, less absenteeism, and less temptation for pilferage.

Good training is an investment in a person with the potential to be a good worker. As a business, we are dependent on people; people producing a good product and people dealing directly with customers. An investment in training each of those people is a key that unlocks our potential to be a successful restaurant owner or manager (Miller and Porter, 1985).

REFERENCES

Miller, Jack E. and Mary Porter. 1985. *Supervision in the Hospitality Industry.* New York: John Wiley and Sons, pp. 142-147.

Forrest, Lewis C., Jr. 1990. *Training for the Hospitality Industry.* East Lansing, MI: Education Institute of the American Hotel and Motel Association, pp. 75-85.

References to Training Plans:

See Miller and Porter, pp. 152 and 153, *The Action Plan,* and pp. 155-158, *The Training Plan.*

See Forrest, pp. 30-36, *Job Breakdown,* and pp. 151-157, *Designing the Training Plan.*

Training Fundamentals

Form 6.1

STANDARD PROCEDURE SHEET

Job: Wait Person   **Unit:** Communicate with Customer

Task No. 2: Explain the Menu

1. Customers will indicate verbally or by behavior when they are ready to place the food order. Approach the table at this time.

2. Explain the daily specials and answer any questions about the food the customers have at this time.

3. Ask if the customers are ready to order. Start with the women when writing the orders. Try to stand at each customer's right as you take the order. Children first, women next, and then the men.

4. Help each person plan a complete meal. Be sensitive to what each person wants. Be knowledgeable about the food: where it is from, what is in season, which items complement and enhance each other, and so forth.

5. Answer questions about preparation methods, tastes, and portion sizes.

6. Inform each guest about the approximate cooking times for the selection.

7. Accurately record selection. If you are not clear or if children are being served, repeat selection to the customer.

8. Courteously explain allowable substitutions. If uncertain, ask manager and then go back and explain to the guest.

9. When customers have completed the order, make one last check to see if anything else is needed.

10. Collect the menus and return them to menu holder.

11. Turn in food orders to the kitchen and begin the serving procedure.

Form 6.2

STANDARD PROCEDURE SHEET

Job: Waiter / Waitress **Unit:** Communicate with Customer

Task No. 3: Guest Check Procedure

1. On guest check, number seats at table.

2. Ask each guest in turn what he or she wants and record following the appropriate seat number.

3. Suggest additional items such as appetizer, soup, salad, beverage, wine, specials.

4. Ask for all "choice of" selections and record on check.

5. Use correct abbreviations.

6. Turn in order to kitchen.

7. Complete guest check with prices.

Attachments:

  Copy of guest check
  Menu abbreviations

Training Fundamentals

Form 6.3

TRAINING PLAN

| **Job:** |
| **Unit:** |
| **Task(s):** |
| **Training Objective:** |

Training Time	**Learning Activities**	**Method**

Materials:

Evaluation of Learning:

Form 6.4

TRAINING PLAN

Job: Waiter / Waitress

Unit: Communicate with Customers

Task(s): No. 2   Explains the Menu
No. 3   Guest Check Procedure

Training Objective: After six hours and thirty minutes of training, the employee will demonstrate the ability to take a food order for a table of four completely and accurately, courteously explaining the menu to the customers and using correct guest check procedures. The menu knowledge will be sufficient for most customer questions, but the trainee will know when the question is more complex and requests information from the manager.

Training Time	Learning Activities	Method
10 Min.	3-Trainee views the whole sequence	Videotape
20 min.	3-Writes seat numbers on guest check	JIT
30 min.	2-Approach the customer	JIT, Role-play
30 min.	2-Explain daily specials	JIT, Role-play
20 min.	2 & 3-Begin taking the order Trainee receives marketing lesson	JIT, Role-play, Videotape
1 hr.	2 & 3-Help customers plan meal	JIT, Role-play
1 hr.	2-Answer questions	JIT, Role-play
20 min.	2-Inform customers of cooking time	JIT, Role-play
30 min.	2 & 3-Record selection	JIT, Role-play
30 min.	2 & 3-Accompanying items	JIT, Role-play
20 min.	2-Allowable substitutions	JIT, Role-play
20 min.	2-One last check	JIT, Role-play
10 min.	2-Collect menus	JIT
20 min.	3-Turn food order into kitchen	JIT
10 min.	3-Complete guest check with prices	JIT

Form 6.4 (continued)

Materials: Illustration of service area in kitchen
List of daily specials
Guest checks
Properly set table with four chairs
Menu
Menu abbreviations
Menu holder
Videotape of wait person taking an order for a table of four
Videotape on suggestive selling

Evaluation of Learning: For a beginning employee without experience, each JIT allows the trainer to see how well the person is learning.

Chapter 7

Training Systems and Aids

By now you can see we think training employees is an important part of the job. Just as you set up a system to produce a meal with menus, recipes, and production schedules, a system for developing trained employees needs to be a part of your operation. Let us look at that training schedule we showed you in Chapter 5 (Form 7.1). You will see Mary and Keith have individual training sessions on nine tenth and nine twelfth. Group training sessions are scheduled for nine tenth, nine eleventh, and nine thirteenth with Mary, Tim, Rachel, Doug, and Jean. We want to talk about both group and individual training methods. We will also explain how to develop your training resources, both written and visual. Sometimes you want to develop your own and sometimes the appropriate material is available from other sources. A training/meeting room is a valuable resource and helps to keep training things available and orderly. The final aspect of training we will talk about in this chapter is how to set up and start a training system and how to keep it running and nourishing for your restaurant.

METHODS OF TRAINING

The two individual methods of training we want to discuss are programmed individualized instruction and coaching and counseling.

Programmed Individualized Instruction

This method of training encourages employees to learn on their own. The learning material is designed to actively involve the learner and the learner receives immediate feedback, which is a critical feature of programmed individualized instruction. The programmed learning can be presented in a variety of the following formats: notebooks, computers, slides and audiotapes, or videotapes. Self-paced learning can keep the self-directed person challenged and it can reduce the frustration for a person who does not learn as quickly as another.

The method involves these following four procedures:

1. The learner reads a statement or problem, studies an illustration, or receives an audio stimulus.

2. The learner makes a response to these stimuli.

3. The learner is then shown immediately whether the response is correct or incorrect.

4. Upon mastering the information, the learner moves on to the next frame of information at her own pace.

The increment of material can be short or long depending upon the type of learner using the material.

The advantages of self-paced instruction are it requires active participation by the learner, minimizes the risk of error, provides immediate feedback, allows the learner to learn at her own pace, and requires no special classroom or equipment.

A disadvantage is that it is not useful for non-self-directed learners or employees who are not motivated.

Coaching and Counseling

One of the advantages of having standards of performance is everyone knows your expectations. As you go through the kitchen and dining area talking to employees, you naturally comment on their work performance, and your comments reinforce your belief in the standards. This movement about the workplace visiting and talking about the work is a form of informal coaching.

A more formal process of coaching and counseling is frequently used when employee performance no longer meets expectations—maybe it is the incorrect preparation of a special salad. This approach for improving performance is used for the fully-trained employee who has demonstrated by past performance an ability to do the job. For some reason current performance has deteriorated.

A conference between you and the employee to establish the reason for the performance problem is called. This should take place in a non-threatening environment where the employee is free to talk and express ideas and feelings. The focus of the conference should be the problem the employee has in performing the job.

When the problem has been established, both you and the employee should agree on how to solve the problem. If there is something in the workplace that is causing a problem, like a broken refrigerator, do what you can to correct the situation. Have the employee set goals that will lead to correction of the problem—the mise en place will match the standard illustrated for the pantry.

At this point, take a minute to think about what good coaching is. We both have granddaughters about the same age and the girls are playing on their first soccer team. They are very young girls and have never played soccer before. One of the fathers (not either of us) gets very excited about the game and constantly yells instructions to his daughter. The coach is very good, patient, teaches fundamentals, and encourages the girls to learn good soccer skills. This father is so intense that he is constantly after his girl during the game.

Good coaches let the players play the game and talk about what is happening when the pace stops. Let the employee with the problem perform, encourage good performance, and have times when you can talk quietly about what is happening.

A note of caution about the counseling part of this combination. Be aware of your own limitations. Sometimes a problem is involved that is beyond your capacity to solve. You can keep a list of community services and provide the employee with names and addresses of people who can help solve difficult problems.

Coaching and counseling is in order whenever you think people will improve themselves. It is a method of encouraging improvement without hovering over people. Discover the problem, set improvement goals, praise when possible, be ready to discuss problems, and put them on their own as much as possible. For the workers who have successfully performed in the past, coaching is the appropriate method to solve a performance problem.

Group Methods

There are several reasons for training your employees by a group presentation rather than a one-on-one method. Human relations training is more effective if it is conducted in groups. An effective way of promoting teamwork is encouraging employees to become involved with group projects. When a new piece of equipment is purchased or a new menu item is introduced, a group session is the best way to let everyone know about it. The continual reinforcement of sanitation and safe work practices works well with a group presentation. A new promotion requires the involvement of everyone and should be explained with a group method.

The process for group training follows the same four training steps that the job instruction training method did: preparation, presentation, trial, and follow-up. The preparation requires the trainees, the training area, and the trainer all be made ready for the training session. The trainer must know the subject matter, the learning materials used to aid instruction, the four steps of training, and the people to be trained. There are two primary methods used for group presentation—information/lecture and participation. The informational method is used to explain policies and update practices. It may be a presentation with a period of questions and answers. It may be a demonstration mixed with some participation by the group.

Information/Lecture

A lecture is the oldest and most commonly used method of instruction. There are some guidelines for this method of instruction. It is used to focus on one idea, issue, or problem. An outline should be used to keep everything to the point and handouts or media as well as questions from the group should be kept within the session objectives. It is critically important the session be kept to an appropriate length—short and sweet. Related to this guideline is concern for the physical factors of ventilation and climate control which must be adequate for the number of people. One of the difficulties of this method is it may not hold the attention of the group.

Participative Methods

People learn in different ways. The key to effective training is to match the method with the person's way of learning. Some people learn best by periods of instruction followed by periods of study and reflection. Others learn best by talking to someone else about what is going on. Participative sessions are ways of having people talk about what they are thinking, but it directs the discussion to the issue at hand. The participative methods are: conference, role-play, group problem solving (quality circles), case study, and discussions. We will give you some guidelines for each of these methods.

A conference involves an expert actively participating with a group. It provides an in-depth study of a topic. Some of the experts available to a restaurant are: wine suppliers, equipment distributors, health department people, or food distributors.

Role-playing is useful in allowing learners to practice skills without the pressure of performance. It should closely portray a real work situation. You have to explain the exercise and the situation involved to the group. The payers are given directions for dialogue and actions while the rest of the group act as observers. A period of feedback and discussion completes the learning activity. Some of the topics that lend themselves to role-play are: how to order food from the kitchen, handling a customer complaint, or employee participation in a promotional activity.

Group problem solving can be useful for showing all the sides of an issue. If the members of a group are open and honest, many different points of view will be expressed. This allows many ideas to be brought out and can stimulate a creative approach to solving a problem. When an employee is present and listens to everyone, the employee better understands the decision, and communication of the decision is simplified.

For a new employee, participation in a problem-solving group would be focused on lower priority activities such as furnishing the employee's break area. As the employee becomes knowledgeable and gains group participation skills, higher priority activities can be the focus. Perhaps you are looking for new menu suggestions, or maybe there is a problem getting orders out of the kitchen in a timely fashion. Skillful employees can generate valuable solutions to solving these problems, and, thus, become committed to having the solutions work.

The use of case studies is similar to role-playing using written situations for discussion. The case study must be realistic and based upon observation of things that occur in the workspace. At the end of the case study, ask questions that relate to the learning objectives for the employees. The group discussing the case study should be comprised of four to six people. Give them time to read the case study, have them discuss answers to the questions, have them report on the groups perceptions and answers, and re-cap the main points relating to what they are learning. The benefits of the case study method are the following: people have an opportunity to share experiences and ideas with the group, learners develop confidence in expressing themselves, and a spirit of acceptance to the group may develop. The problem may be that someone tries to dominate the discussion. Establish a rule that everyone talks once before someone speaks a second time. A case study might be written about receiving procedures or a recurring sanitation or safety behavioral problem.

Directed group discussions involve a group of people gathering to discuss a topic interesting to them. A trainer prepares the group by providing informative material about the topic. This may be reading material, a videotape, a demonstration, or even a short lecture presentation. The group leader should encourage everyone to make a comment on the topic, keep the group on track, avoid arguments, ask thought provoking questions, close the topic when appropriate, and summarize. Some topics that lend themselves to discussion could be using a new piece of equipment, opening a new section or department in the restaurant, participating in a community project or celebration, or even how the restaurant can participate in recycling activities.

DEVELOPING A SYSTEM

Do you remember when you first began driving a car? You had to think about everything you did. It was only after much practice your driving skills became responsive and reflexes reactive to the situation. When you put a training system in place, it takes great effort and concentration about every part of the system. Once it is in place, it is a useful vehicle for developing valuable human resources and responding to the competitive situation.

We hope this book enables you to develop materials for training people for your operation. We have talked about setting standards for your business, writing job descriptions, writing job procedure sheets and manuals, doing job analyses, job breakdown, and training plans. All of these are critical elements for training employees. The key to productivity is to put all of these elements into a system that works for your operation.

Think of the training schedule (Form 7.1) as a road map. It is a visual guide that helps you to see the direction of your training program. Like any path that you follow, it requires great concentration in the beginning, but when it becomes a habit, you are able to observe the immediate situation and respond with the appropriate training elements. Your training schedule gives you a way to adapt to your business needs.

The Instructor

When your business is large enough to have a training system, you will have to share the role of trainer with other people. In our story about on-the-job training for Carol, we said that Jerry and Pat were the best people on their shift to do the training. We have said the qualities of a good trainer are knowledge of the job, knowing how to train, and having a good attitude. In your system of training, you want to develop those qualities within some of your people. Ideally, all your employees have the correct feeling about customer relations, product quality, and sanitation. The job knowledge has been developed by performing the job. When you are thinking about developing the qualities of a good trainer, you want to develop the knowledge of how to train and the skills of how to train. These skills are closely related to the adult learning process and the job instruction training method.

The following is a list of training tips that have proven to be valuable aids in getting organized:

1. **Know your trainees.** This the value of a pretest. You want to teach what the trainee needs to know to perform the job according to your standards.

2. **Prepare for instruction.** Have everything ready: training materials, the place of instruction, and the training plan or lesson plan for that session.

3. **Teach in the order performed.** This relates to the preparation for instruction. Know exactly what is to be taught, how much time it takes to teach the lesson, the steps in the operations, the features and key points of each step, and the proper order. You do not want to forget something and have to backtrack and lose the sequence of performance.

4. **Teach small units.** Each unit of instruction should be the appropriate size for the learner. If a step is troublesome, it may be necessary to divide the step into two or more smaller steps.

5. **Teach the entire operation.** When performing a job through habit, it is easy to forget parts of the operation. Be careful to include all fundamental information and important connecting links.

6. **Know key points of operation.** By stressing the things that make or break an operation, the instructor focuses the trainee's concentration on what is important.

7. **Explain why it is done a certain way.** Telling why a job is performed a certain way helps the learner make connections with what is important about the task and helps put the task into an area of interest for the learner.

8. **Use descriptive specific words.** Choose appropriate words that are descriptive of the particular tasks. Explain the terminology that is used in your restaurant.

9. **Be patient with the trainee.** Remember you know the subject and the job well; the trainee does not. Everyone learns at

a different rate and instruction should be paced for the learner. A patient, helpful attitude by the instructor helps to facilitate learning.

The instructor is the person who drives your training system. This is the crucial element.

Resources

In a restaurant, we think of raw food supplies as resources that are processed to become marketable finished products. We search the food markets to find just the right food items for our operation. With the size of the industry and the economic impact of restaurants, there are many suppliers that are working to provide just the right food or beverage item for an individual restaurant. When we are talking about training, we are talking about human resources. Training enables our employees to develop and becomes an important part of how we face our market. There are also suppliers working to provide resources to help train and develop the restaurant employee. First, let us talk about written resources.

Written

The purpose of this book is to get you to write your own materials. This gives you control and helps you work through exactly what is needed for your unique operation. When we wrote this book, the first chapter written was chapter 3, Job Standards. Setting standards of performance must be a first priority.

Communicating those standards of performance is what training is all about. Job breakdowns, procedure sheets, and training plans will give you the necessary resources for good training sessions.

The time required to complete this book was more than two years as we were both involved with many other things. We recognize writing your own training materials is time consuming. While you are preparing training materials, use other available training resources. Appendix A contains a list of publishers who have materials related to restaurant training. Remember, you must be clear in your own mind about the standards of product quality and customer service needed for your customers and your operation.

Seminars

The National Restaurant Association has excellent seminars on a variety of topics focused on the food service industry. The seminars are conducted by recognized authorities in specific areas. The written materials and workbooks included with the price of the seminars provide you with practical information that can help you work through particular problems in your operation.

To obtain a brochure of current offerings write:

National Restaurant Association
The Educational Foundation
250 South Wacker Drive, Suite 1400
Chicago, IL 60606-5834

Video/Movies

Video can be used effectively to demonstrate technique, convey information, supplement, and reinforce other training presentations. Videos should be short and to the point reinforcing main points of learning. Video is certainly a common media for employees and if a video can be used regularly for training in your restaurant, it can be a worthwhile purchase. A list of companies who have videotapes available for the food service industry may be found in Appendix A.

Slides

One of the problems with purchasing a video is that your people may resist training shown in a kitchen or dining area nothing like yours and with equipment they do not have. Slides are simple, low-cost training tools that can be taken in your operation. The benefit of slides is the trainer can focus on one aspect of a task for as long as needed to convey the information. Slides can be an effective training tool for both group and individual learning. The drawback to using slides is they work best in a dark room and this makes it difficult to take notes.

Overhead Projectors and Transparencies

An effective visual aid for group learning that can be used in a fully-lighted room is the overhead projector. The preparation of transparencies to use on the overhead projector is relatively inexpensive. One cost estimate is approximately $2.50 per transparency.

Printed words on a transparency should be large and legible. There should be no more than six or seven words per line and no more than six or seven lines per transparency. Written material should be on the vertical format, and graphs or illustrations on the horizontal format. When using the overhead projector, turn it off after each use. People will focus on the light and not give full attention to what is being said.

Media and visual aids add variety to a presentation and help hold the attention of the learner. Media should never control the presentation but should enhance the learning experience. You want to be sure the message from the media is translated by the learner into a learning experience and good performance of job skills.

Preview all media (video, slides, audiotapes, or transparencies) to be sure they relate well to your workers and your operation. Also, check to be sure the equipment works.

Training Room

There are some types of training that do not occur within the work areas. A training room can be a valuable resource for improving the quality of training. The size of the room will depend upon the space available at the restaurant location. Generally, a rectangular room is best. The primary requirement for an effective training room is everyone in the room must be able to see and hear the presentation. You usually want training to occur close to the workplace. It especially helps new employees so they can see other workers and the place they will be working, and begin to sense the spirit of teamwork in the workplace. Check for adequate heat, air conditioning, and ventilation. It is surprising how quickly people doze off in a stuffy room. A bookcase and a cabinet that can be locked will provide convenient storage space for training materials and equipment. Make sure someone takes the responsibility to see these things are kept orderly, current, and in good working condition. Checklist 7.1 provides things to consider for a training room.

IMPLEMENTATION AND MAINTENANCE OF A TRAINING SYSTEM

The goal for a training system is consistent employee performance at good levels of productivity, customer satisfaction, and employee fulfillment. A training system needs: clear objectives; a master plan for training outlining the instructor, the materials, and the methods; consistent evaluation of plan effectiveness; and a measurement of results as it relates to your standards of productivity, customer satisfaction, and employee fulfillment.

Training Objectives

Objectives are set by analyzing the student. Who is to be trained? Some of the questions to answer when training objectives are being set are:

Training Systems and Aids   7-11

Checklist 7.1

TRAINING ROOM CHECKLIST

1. Can everyone see and hear?

2. Where are the heating, air conditioning, and ventialtion controls?

3. Are the wall recepticles adapted for three pronged plugs?

4. Is the power for visual projectors on the same circuit as room lights?

5. Is all equipment working?

6. Will you need an extension cord?

7. Can the lighting be controlled to dim or darken the room?

8. Are the chairs reasonably comfortable?

9. Do you need special provisions for people with disabilities?

10. Is threre adequate aisle space?

11. Is there adequate space for trainees to write notes?

12. Can charts, illustrations, or other training materials be hung on the wall?

13. Are there any open windows and glaring lights that may be distracting?

14. Are there any ringing telephones or other noises nearby that may be distracting?

15. Are exit doors at the back of the room?

16. Is threre space for a coffee break in the room, or nearby?

17. Are ashtrays, water glasses, water pitchers, and waste baskets available?

18. Is there a place to hang coats?

19. Do you need any of the following: name cards, writing tablets, pencils, pencil sharpner, three-hole punch paper, paper clips, rubber bands, stapler, staples, staple remover, scissors?

Are these new employees?

Do they have previous experience?
>	What skills and knowledge do they possess?
>	What skills and knowledge are they lacking?

Are you training present employees for another job?
>	What skills and knowledge do they need for the new job?
>	What skills and knowledge are they lacking?

Has something changed in the workplace—menu, equipment, procedure?
>	What training is needed for the employee to adapt to the change?

Training objectives are determined by subtracting what the person knows from what the person needs to know and then teaching the result of this equation. For example, a new wait person may need to learn your method of writing the guest check, your method of ordering food from the kitchen, and your method of selling wines. The new wait person may already know the correct table set-up and how to serve food and beverages. The training objectives for this person relates to your standard of performance for the unit of work and reflects your standard for the time required to learn this unit of work. A training objective for this new wait person might read as follows: Bob will be able to take the food order for a table of six with 100 percent accuracy within ten minutes. Bob will learn to do this with one hour of classroom instruction, one day of on-the-job instruction and one week of practice.

The Master Plan for Training

The master plan for training relates to the types of training that are needed and the objectives of the training. For example, the instructor for Bob's classroom training will be Bob's immediate supervisor and the instructor for Bob's on-the-job training will be another wait person. The instructor for the one week of practice will again be Bob's supervisor. Some of the questions to be answered about the instructors when developing the master plan for training are:

> What type of training is needed?
>
> Will there be general information that applies to everyone, like dress and grooming?
>
> Will there be more specific skill training?
>
> Among the employees with expert knowledge, who has the qualities of a good trainer?

Training Systems and Aids

What is the cost factor for a particular instructor?
Is there an outside expert who will be a good trainer?

Materials

Selection of materials also depends upon all the objectives of the master plan for training. For example, Bob needs to see the correct abbreviations used for each menu item if he is learning how to write the guest check. A guest check procedures sheet will be the basis for the training plan for this particular skill. It is the instructor's responsibility to see all training materials are on hand. Some of the questions to be answered about training materials when developing the master training plan are:

What materials are available for training?
Does our training manual have a written training plan for this skill?
Is there a written procedures sheet available for this skill?
Will an outside expert have handout material?
Do we have slides or videos that are focused on what needs to be learned?
Does the employee handbook have information about something the trainees need to know?
Does the sanitation manual or safety manual have information about something the trainees need to know?
Will it help the trainees to see the recipe for a menu item?
Is there money in the training budget to produce specific material?
What types of equipment are involved?
What is the cost factor for the use of particular learning materials?

The methods to be used for training depend upon the number and type of students and the learning objectives for these students. Some limitations will be placed upon the choice of a method by the physical facilities available and the requirements of the jobs of each of the trainees. There are three basic methods for presenting learning experiences. Usually some combination of these three methods is used. One method is on-the-job training where the person learns by following a qualified trainer and performing tasks under the watchful eye of this trainer. Another method is the lecture/demonstration method of presenting information. This can be for a group, one-on-one, or self-study instruction. This method is used to explain policy and to update and reinforce practices. This method works best when it is combined with one of the other methods, on-the-job practice, or participation. The third method is participation. Some participation techniques are question and answer sessions, role-play, case studies, trial performance, and small group discussion.

Some of the questions to ask about the methods to be used for a master plan for training are:

> Will job conditions permit effective use of the method?
> What is the cost factor of a particular method?
> Is the chosen instructor able to use the method?
> Will the trainees accept the method of instruction?
> Will the method bring about the desired results?
> Will the method help meet the training objectives?

Implementation of the Master Plan for Training

The worksheets for the training master plan should be tablet paper. On the first sheet of paper, list the names of the trainees and the training objectives for each person. These objectives must be very specific and must relate to the performance standards set for each job. Indicate your choice of an instructor for each student.

The training materials sheet should be a printed sheet listing all the training materials you have available for your operation. List the training manuals, job manuals, and operations manuals that are available. List operations equipment that can be used for training and the employee handbook manual. List sets of transparencies, slide presentations, and video training tapes. For materials that are on a computer disk, list the commands that bring up the menu to retrieve the appropriate text. The instructors will be able to check the materials needed from this printed sheet to prepare the necessary instructional materials.

The worksheet for the selection of the method should allow for some problem solving techniques. You want to answer the question, "What is the best and cheapest way to enable these people to be competently trained?" One major factor affecting the selection of a method is time. How much time does the employee have for training and how much time does the instructor have to train? If you have written training plans, these will tell you the time required to reach the learning objectives. If you do not have a written training plan, you need to make an estimate of the time required. Now look at the time allocated for training on your training schedule. This will tell you how much time is available for the demonstration of a technique and how much time can be allowed for the trainees to try the demonstrated technique or how much time can be given to role-play or group discussion.

A problem solving technique that may help you decide the best method to use is to write down all the benefits of using a particular method on one side of the paper and write down all the weaknesses of using a particular method on the other side of the paper. Make your decision on which method best fits the situation.

When you have selected the method to be used, list the method with the name of the trainer and the trainee's learning objectives. The master plan for training worksheets will be back-up documentation for the training schedule. The training schedule (Form 7.1) will be prepared weekly, or at least monthly, listing when training is to occur, who will be trained, how the training is to take place, what will be the content of the training, and who is responsible for providing the training.

Evaluation

One of the rules of thumb for management states that you get what you inspect. For any system to continue, there must be feedback on what is happening. Does the training system enable the employees to be productive, have customer service orientation, and be reasonably satisfied with the work and the job?

Frequent testing during the process of learning gives feedback to both the instructor and the trainee. The trainee can see where help is needed and seek out proper instruction. The instructor can be flexible with time, materials, and methods to meet the demonstrated need for learning. Learning will take place only when the trainee wants to learn. The evaluation process should be open enough for the trainee to talk about what kinds of problems are occurring on the job and what kinds of training will be helpful.

A formal method of evaluation demonstrates an interest in the learning process, gives the learner a chance to demonstrate an ability to learn, and reinforces the learning experience. Both written and performance tests should be used. The written tests can be questions and answers, a written report of what was learned, or a reaction to the learning experience.

A formal evaluation and a reward at the conclusion of a training program shows respect for the training, the instructor, and the person who is being trained.

One of the most important results of passing an evaluation test is an increase in self-esteem. It has been proven that a person with satisfying learning experiences is strongly motivated to return for more learning experiences. The evaluation is a critical step in the training process.

Measurement of Results

The true evaluation of a training system is how well the person performs on the job. Chapter 8 deals with budgeting as a means of setting standards and measuring results. The final chapter, chapter 9, talks about employee appraisal programs as an evaluation of the training program. We will also show you some forms that can be used to evaluate the performance of your staff.

These forms are used for guest rating, management rating, or peer rating of the performance of restaurant employees. There are a variety of formats available. The sheets shown here may or may not fit your operation. You may want to develop a format that best suits your operation. These are good samples.

REFERENCES

Miller, Jack E. and Mary Porter. 1985. *Supervision in the Hospitality Industry.* New York: John Wiley and Sons, Inc., pp. 277-285.

This, Leslie E. 1979. *The Small Meeting Planner.* Houston, TX: Gulf Publishing Co., pp. 85 and 86. This book has practical suggestions for planning meeting rooms and holding effective meetings.

Training Systems and Aids

Form 7.1

TRAINING SCHEDULE

Employee / Average Training Time	Linens Tom 30 Min	Tilting Skillet Hobart 2 Hours	Hostess Tom Maria 8 Hours	Order Food Kathy 4 Hours	Dress / Grooming Film 1 Hour
1. Mary	9/11		9/10-9/17		9/13 a.m.
2. Keith		9/10		9/12-9/13	
3. Tim	9/11				9/13
4. Rachael	9/11				9/13
5. Doug		9/10			9/13
6. Jean		9/10			9/13

Training Times:
    Tuesday and Wednesday 9:00–10:30 a.m.
    Monday, Wednesday, and Thursday 1:30–3:30 p.m.

Unless you are notified otherwise, training sessions will begin promptly at 9:00 in the morning or 1:30 in the afternoon.

Chapter 8

Labor Control

Training is an important part of the ability to control labor costs. If training methods are effective, we are able to set standards of productivity and our people are able to meet the quality and quantity standards. Monitoring labor costs is one of the indirect ways we evaluate a training system.

LABOR COST

Probably two of the most critical problems that face us today as people in the restaurant industry are 1) Getting people to work, and 2) The cost of those people once they come to work. We have talked about the problems involved in recruiting, selecting, and training people. In this chapter, we want to talk about factors that influence the cost of paying these people to work for us.

One factor that influences our ability to control labor costs is an inability to mechanize our work. Can you imagine how you would feel after a day of work if you went to your favorite local eating place looking for some neighborly friendliness, and a robot appeared to take your order? First, you would think it was a joke. Eventually, you would realize the awful truth and the depressing realization of another non-human encounter would sink in. We want somebody serving that food. We want a human there talking to us in a personal, one-on-one encounter. We need human presence.

We talked about the problems caused by our changing demographics and shrinking labor force. Every fast-food marquee we pass has a "Now Hiring, All Shifts" message. When the supply of workers decrease, the competition, for workers increases. With increased competition, we have to pay more just to have them accept our open position. One of the most expensive items we face is the cost of labor, which in many cases exceeds food costs.

Labor costs are influenced by management, training, and scheduling. If these three elements are effective, our labor costs will remain a reasonable portion of our total expense picture. When we discuss labor costs, we usually talk in terms of the percentage of sales. Labor cost is defined as the amount that you spend for all labor, all benefits and fringes of labor. A ratio is derived by taking your total sales divided into the cost of labor. This will give the labor cost percentage. It is always an expression in relationship to sales for the organization. When this percentage is reasonable, you will make a profit. When the percentage is not reasonable, you will not make a profit. Let's look at some of the management and scheduling factors that influence labor costs.

ESTIMATING LABOR INTO THE BUDGET

In order to estimate labor for the restaurant, it is necessary to forecast future business. Let us look at the following five critical factors for forecasting:

1. Forecasting represents the thinking of all the people with knowledge of facts affecting the work load. Everybody who knows anything about it gets in and talks about it.

2. Forecasting should contain as much information as possible to help with staff planning.

3. The forecast should be prepared enough time in advance to permit people to plan accurately.

4. There should be a verbal discussion of the forecast by those who prepare it and the people that use it so that there can be some give and take or some discussion of the plan.

5. There should be a mechanism for correcting your forecast and notifying people in charge of scheduling so they may schedule correctly and effectively.

When I was in operations, some of my supervisors and myself had lunch together at about 1:00 in the afternoon, where we would have a forecast meeting. We talked about the numbers of parties we had the next day and the outside groups who were going to be on campus. We then made our plans for production for the number of people coming in the next day. At that point, we would say, "Look, we don't have any of this, we can't get any of that, take that off the menu, change this, change that, add these people and hours to the schedule." We found this to be a very effective way. It is not a scientific method, but it worked well for us in that particular operation.

You may have weekly or daily meetings to go over the expected business for the next week or the next day. That is a method of forecasting. It is not a scientific or even a quasi-scientific forecast, but it is a method of forecasting. Once you have done this forecast, regardless of what method, then use a systematic method of scheduling people to fit with the amount of business and the fluctuations of business that you expect. Begin to outline or establish a known cost for your work schedule and then translate this information into schedules for individuals. This is what we mean by control of labor. The schedule and the forecast are control mechanisms.

CALCULATION OF LABOR COSTS

Table 8.1 shows a method of forecasting labor using the labor cost percentage. This labor forecast is based on past sales of $2,000. This is a known volume of business that we have done. Then we begin to divide up where we spent our labor and amounts of money. We have a certain amount that we have spent on cooks, wait persons, dishwashers, buspeople, and other kitchen help. This is all based

Table 8.1

9/24 Sales $2,000
Cooks	100
Other Kitchen	75
Dishwasher	25
Wait People	75
Bus People	50
Total	325

Department Labor to Total Labor Ratio:
Cooks	100 ÷ 325 = 31%
Other Kitchen	75 ÷ 325 = 23%
Dishwasher	25 ÷ 325 = 7.7%
Wait People	75 ÷ 325 = 23%
Bus People	50 ÷ 325 = 15.3%

Department Labor to Sales Ratio:
Cooks	100 ÷ 2,000 = 5%
Other Kitchen	75 ÷ 2,000 = 3.75%
Dishwasher	25 ÷ 2,000 = 1.25%
Wait People	75 ÷ 2,000 = 3.75%
Bus People	50 ÷ 2,000 = 2.5%

upon the history of $2,000 in past sales. We begin to establish a percentage of each job function to total labor cost. Of this amount of money, $2,000, we have spent $100 for our cooks. For wait people, we have spent $75, dishwashers $25, buspeople $50. For other kitchen personnel we have spent $75 for a total of $325.

Then we calculate a percentage of each function to total labor. These are the amounts that we have spent:

- Percentage to total would be 31 percent (100 divided by 325) for cooks.
- Percentage to total would be 23 percent (75 divided by 325) for wait people.
- Percentage to total would be 7.69 percent (25 divided by 325) for dishwashers.
- Percentage to total would be 15.3 percent (50 divided by 325) for buspeople.
- Percentage to total would be 23 percent (75 divided by 325) for others.
- Total of these percentages equals 99 percent.

Then we calculate the percentage to sales:

- 100 divided by 2,000 = 5 percent.
- 75 divided by 2,000 = 3.75 percent.
- 25 divided by 2,000 = 1.25 percent.
- 50 divided by 2,000 = 2.5 percent.
- 75 divided by 2,000 = 3.75 percent.

The total of these percentages equals a labor cost of 16.25 percent (which is really pretty low).

This is based on $2,000 of volume. Now we are going to forecast our volume for September 25 (Table 8.2). We have a forecasted volume of $3,000. (This $3,000 came from the last forecast meeting

---

Table 8.2

9/25 Forecast Sales $3,000
Labor Cost Percentage Standards:

Cooks	5%
Other Kitchen	3.75%
Dishwashers	1.25%
Wait People	3.75%
Bus People	2.5%

Cooks	5% x 3,000 = $	150.00
Other Kitchen	3.75% x 3,000 =	112.50
Dishwashers	1.25% x 3,000 =	37.50
Wait People	3.75% x 3,000 =	112.50
Bus People	2.5% x 3,000 =	75.00

where this amount was estimated.) How much can I spend in labor for cooks, waiters, buspeople and other kitchen help? I must go through and calculate my anticipated or forecasted sales as follows:

- ◊ For cooks it is 5 percent of $3,000 or $150.
- ◊ For wait people it is 3.75 percent of $3,000 or $112.50.
- ◊ For dishwashers it is 1.25 percent of $3,000 or $37.50.
- ◊ For buspeople it is 2.5 percent of $3,000 or $75.00.
- ◊ For others it is 3.75 percent of $3,000 or $112.50.

One thing that is really critical when doing this is that the service has been satisfactory and the standards we have set have been met. Do not sacrifice standards to save labor cost. You can always do it cheaper but it may affect sales and customer satisfaction.

ESTABLISHING REALISTIC STANDARDS

In the past, one problem with our labor forecasting and scheduling has been our view of scheduling unskilled or semi-skilled workers. We tend to think, "I need one, but I will bring in two because it does not cost a whole lot." We are in a position where we cannot do that today. The numbers of people just are not there. We do not have a huge pool of people to pull from anymore. The big labor pool that we have had in the past is not available. A major objective for the manager is the maximum utilization of the labor that is available. The present cost of labor and final profit needs prevents casual use of labor money.

In forecasting and labor planning, one of the things that is absolutely critical is to establish a norm or a standard for all the people who work for you. Chapter 3 explains how to set standards of performance. If you are able to tell someone what you want done and how you want it done, you establish a standard or a norm for that person. As a manager, you have to establish what is going to be the standard of performance. What is the norm for the people who work for you? You have to train them, lead them, and teach them to do the job according to your standards.

Excessive staffing creates careless work habits and high labor costs. Inadequate staff impairs the proper function of the restaurant. At the Marriott Hotel, you could schedule one room service waiter for a house count of 600 people, but you would not meet the established standard of service. One person could not do that amount of work over that period of time.

A calculation to determine the number of units of output per employee can be made based on past sales history. This can give you a baseline for planning the work load for each employee. The calculation is as follows: divide the number of the units of output by the number of employees.

$$\frac{\text{Units of Output}}{\text{Number of Employees}}$$

You can take any output you want to measure the productivity; the number of salads, the number of entrees, or the number of customers. Then take the number of workers in that unit and divide it into the output. This will give you a unit of productivity per worker. Let's say we are going to work in the pantry. My pantry produces 180 salads, and I have two pantry workers.

$$\frac{180 \text{ Salads}}{2 \text{ Pantry Worker}}$$

That would give a unit of productivity of 90 for each worker. Just as when we calculate based on a percentage of sales, it is critical the salads have been satisfactory and our standards of quality and service have been met.

Table 8.3 shows the calculation for the number of customers served and the number of employees in each department. This calculation shows one cook can produce for 100 people and a waitress can produce for 50 people. If everyone is happy and all require-

---

Table 8.3 Productivity Calculation

Date _____ Meal _____ Lunch _____ Customer Count 200 _____

Kitchen Workers	Calculation	Productivity
Lead Cook	200 ÷ 2 Cooks	100
Backup Cook	200 ÷ 2 Cooks	100
Pantry		200
Pots and Pans		200
Dish Room	200 ÷ 2 Workers	100
Dish Room	200 ÷ 2 Workers	100
TOTAL:	200 ÷ 6	33.3

Dining Room

Hostess		200
Waitress	200 ÷ 4 Waitresses	50
Waitress	200 ÷ 4	50
Waitress	200 ÷ 4	50
Waitress	200 ÷ 4	50
Busperson	200 ÷ 2 Bus People	100
Busperson	200 ÷ 2	100
TOTAL:	200 ÷ 7	28.5
Restaurant Total:	200 ÷ 13	15.3

ments have been satisfied for quality, speed, and profit, then we can use the results of this productivity report to calculate the number of people needed for future business.

Almost everything in forecasting is a mathematical calculation. The unfortunate thing is the mathematical computation is not necessarily perfect. It has to entail some of your own experience. For instance, you know this is a slow cook, this waitress spends a lot of time relating to her customers, this pantry person likes to add an artistic touch, or this busperson is really meticulous.

Constructing a Gantt Chart

One of the most helpful tools we have found for scheduling workers and the work they should be doing is a Gantt chart. The Gantt chart answers the question "when." When scheduling people to do a lot of different activities, coordination is important so workers do not waste time. Have you ever scheduled dishwashers to start work at 7:00 and then have them stand around until 8:30 waiting for dirty dishes? You do not want workers to waste time waiting to use a piece of equipment, the arrival of ingredients from a delivery truck, or the completion of someone else's work. Scheduling can be complicated.

The information needed to complete a Gantt chart is what is to be done and a standard of time for each activity. In preparing a Gantt chart, activities are listed in the order in which they are performed. This is the information developed on the job breakdown worksheet in chapter 3. You must figure out how long each activity will take. For example, how long does it take for your salad person to make the tossed green salad? A Gantt chart is a timeline made in graph form with each vertical row of squares representing one time unit. We have used 30-minute increments in our worksheets.

Think about how the workday begins. Who is the first person to arrive and what are the activities that open your business? Use the vertical lines to list the name of the workers. Then begin listing their activities in 30-minute increments horizontally across the graph. You must be able to set priorities for each of the activities. Which ones must be performed first? When must each activity be finished?

A completed Gantt chart shows you how long an entire job takes, what part is being done at any given time, and who is doing it. You will be able to see at a glance what is being done at any moment and exactly when each part of the work should be finished. You will be able to see what work will be done next and when equipment and supplies need to be available for the worker.

We have given you two worksheets (Forms 8.1 and 8.2). One worksheet reflects the typical four-hour meal service work times 10 a.m.–2 p.m. or 4 p.m.–8 p.m. The other reflects an eight-hour worksheet of 7 a.m.–3 p.m. or 3 p.m.–11 p.m. showing preparation time, closing time, and the service time for the meals.

We have filled in one eight-hour Gantt Chart as an example (Form 8.3). This is only a sample. You need to work out a Gantt Chart to fit your operation. Many restaurants find they must schedule employees in four-hour shifts, and you may find four-hour scheduling more appropriate for your operation.

SCHEDULING FOR PRODUCTIVITY

Ideally, as our people gain skills and confidence, they would increase their productivity and thereby earn an increase in wages. This increase in productivity would give you the ability to pay them more money and not increase the labor cost percentage of your business. Unfortunately, the idea of productivity gains in our industry have not been reflected by the numbers. In many cases, there have been decreases in the productivity of the volume that is done by people who are paid more money. Increased wages have not generated that much productivity of the people who work for us. It means that if we do not have a gain in productivity, then we have to realize some other method of transferring productivity to some other aspect of our business. The people who have done the greatest job in the world on this are fast-food people. They have transferred the aspect of service onto the customer. Whenever you can transfer any aspect of service over to the customer, it will increase the productivity of the employees. The biggest problem we have is the inability of management to adjust to ever-increasing costs of labor, and they are ever-increasing.

We are not the same as a manufacturing concern in the food service industry. You have to understand what we are doing is selling an experience to the people who come in to eat and dine with us. We are a service industry and generally speaking, labor is the largest cost ingredient in any service industry. Service does not produce goods that can be stored. Each non-productive work hour represents a direct loss of productivity.

One difficult thing about trying to schedule workers in our industry is that the work load demand is very uneven. It has peaks and valleys during the day and particular days during the week are heavy or slow. There are even heavy and slow patterns for certain months. This is extremely important to use in scheduling people to recognize how the work load distribution changes. When we talk about personnel tables, distribution of work load, and so forth, we have to be aware of the variations and demand for the product which we serve.

We have to set up our production standards based on units of output, which is what we just talked about. Divide your staff into two different types of workers that are classified as fixed or variable staff. The fixed staff will not vary with the volume. There are certain people who must be present all the time. The variable staff should be varied directly with changes in the volume or work load. The chef, maitre d', steward, cashier, and host/hostess are examples of fixed staff. Waiters, buspeople, dishwashers, and pantry people are examples of varied staff because they vary with the number of people expected.

We do two types of scheduling. We do one called a stacked schedule and another called a staggered schedule. The stacked schedule is one where everyone comes to work and leaves at the same time. There are very few operations that truly lend themselves to this rigid application. It is a traditional means of scheduling and, for lack of somebody making a change, will stay in operation that way forever. One of the problems with this schedule is that everyone arrives at the same time and stands around talking. During shift changes, a major problem is just to get them started working.

The staggered system enables employees to arrive at various starting times. The staggered configuration generally results in the same work load with fewer employees. It reduces the idle time at the start of the shift. It minimizes the loss of worker momentum and will recognize variations in patterns of volume. You bring people in when you are busy and recognize the variations in volume. It also reduces the need for overtime by providing somebody at straight time for hours where you might have needed somebody for overtime. It has the potential for reducing the total number of employees. To be effective, you should have the least number of employees to carry out the work program.

Part-time people are used extensively in many areas of the food industry, especially the fast-food industry. If you use part-time people, you get a break on minimum wage by using student employees and avoid providing fringe benefits. You want to center part-time people around peak times of the operation with your core full-time people. Part-time people are very valuable aspects of what we are doing in labor procurement. In today's market, incentives may have to be offered to attract and keep part-time employees.

A split shift schedule is sometimes used but I do not know if you can get people to work them anymore. I am most familiar with an area of St. Louis that uses split shifts. The "Hill" area is filled with neighborhood bars and restaurants. People live there; they work lunch, go home, and come back to work dinner. This is not done much anymore because people are not willing to work that way.

Another element of the schedule is how to schedule days off. They should be scheduled to fit the fluctuations of business activity. You should have some key personnel scheduled on your weekends when your management team is reduced. In some restaurants, during slack time there will not be a manager there at all. When this happens, nobody is in charge. This is often the result of not being able to get someone to work some of the less attractive hours. This should be changed. Hotels use a person designated as a Manager on Duty. One of the problems we have in scheduling is laziness. We get a schedule done and we just stay with it because it is there and it is easy to use—it never changes even though it may be costing us in overtime. You need to look at it in terms of hours, staggered startings, days off, split shifts, or use of part-time people. Begin to establish what you want to do to assign starting time and days off to employees.

Another thing to consider is scheduling vacation time. Vacation is generally a regular part of your payroll. Vacation is normally scheduled for the convenience of employees although it should be scheduled for the business'. A cafeteria company in Kansas City had serious volume declines because of winter weather. It lost money in January, February, and March every year and finally determined it was because of lost volume—nobody went out to eat in winter weather and storm conditions. Yet the restaurant had the same dollar amount for labor. Due to this, it began putting people on vacations in January and February, and made a profit the next year. People do not always like being told when they can take vacations but you have to look out for the business. You need to move away from the traditional practice that everyone goes on vacation in the summer. Volume of business is the determining factor.

PERSONNEL REQUIREMENT GUIDE

Staff requirements are often defined in the terms of work units to be produced. The basic staffing table is the beginning of a payroll control system. It has to indicate the units per day, per hour, or whatever is a reasonable expectation of people at a standard established by management. The second thing is a manager will establish the standard of service. You will serve from the left, from the right, while you are singing, or whatever, but the manager establishes the standards of service. Establish the number of people needed based on numbers of units and standard of service. Those are two of the prerequisites you have in any establishment of a personnel requirement guide.

For example, you have $150 to spend for cooks with a $3,000 expected sales volume. It is your job to distribute that $150 over the

Labor Control

hours the restaurant is open. Over a period of time, you establish that if you have from 0-50 people in a meal, period you need one cook. If you have 50-125, you will need 1.5 cooks. If you have 125-200, you will need two cooks. This is how we develop personnel charts showing what is needed for each position based upon the volume of business. This guide should be customized for your own business. Table 8.4 is an example of a personnel requirement guide. Again, this is just a sample. You want a personnel requirement guide that reflects your operation.

PHYSICAL FACTORS

As we look at the Personnel Requirement Guide, one of the things to concentrate on is the layout of the station. There are a number of establishments that are so illogically laid out that you will never be effective in planning labor. We worked on the plans for the student union at Mizzou and then built it. When we built it, we discovered that the aisle was six inches too wide from the grill to the service counter. The person who was grill cook had to turn and take a half step to set the plate up. So you think about it and decide that all we have to do is move the grill over there so that you simply set up the product to the wait staff. But we analyzed the cost involved in moving the hood, grill refrigeration, and so forth, and calculated that we would have to be in business for some 2,000 years to pay for the modification of this change. There are some times you know what the problem is but know it is not feasible to pay the price to change it.

Look at any equipment in any kitchen and decide what you can do to make the labor situation better than it might be. What about increasing mobility of equipment by putting it on a cart to move it around to where it is used? There are some other things you can do that will assist you in moving things to where you need them without major costs being involved. Sometimes the cost will prohibit whatever it may be. Look at which people use the machines in your kitchen. It may be you need to put that machine on a cart and move it to the person

Table 8.4 Personnel Requirement Guide

Number of Covers	Cooks	Dish People	Other Kitchen	Wait Staff	Bus People
1–50	1.0	1.0	2.0	2.0	1.0
50–125	1.5	1.5	2.5	5.0	1.0
125–200	2.0	2.0	3.0	8.0	2.0
200–275	2.5	2.5	3.5	11.0	3.0
275–350	3.0	3.0	4.0	14.0	3.5

who uses the machine. We will find that one of the labor saving devices we have are probably in the mobility of equipment. It is done this way opposed to the logical layout many times. Sometimes stoves are on wheels so that they can move around rather than changing the layout to aid the labor situation.

Another factor in the efficient use of labor is principles that were developed years ago by a man named Gilbreth. Gilbreth developed 17 principles of motion economy that were based upon a maximum amount of production with a minimum amount of fatigue. Eight of these principles are important and critical to the food service industry.

Arranging the Work within the Proper Work Area

Every human, regardless of build has a maximum horizontal and vertical plane of working. It is best to arrange the work effectively inside this area. Those of you who have tended bar at a catered event have seen what it is like to work on a six- or eight-foot table that is roughly about six inches too low for the normal human. When we did a party we would take four #10 cans of food products and put them under the legs of the table. That would bring it up to a comfortable height for working. If you take your ice out of a 20 or 30 gallon trash can, after it goes down six or eight inches from the top, you have to start bending to get the remaining ice. So, if you put the can on a plastic milk carton, it solves the problem. I gave you the example of Columbia where the counters were too far apart. What you have to do is find a way to solve the problem rather than redesigning the whole kitchen. There are things you can do that will work out for you in developing the limited facilities that you may have.

Pre-position the Tools or Materials

They should be located in the normal area where you work. When we set up a banquet, we pre-position by having one person set up the salad for 200 or 500. It is a very simple thing to do. We use an accordion type cart that is found in many kitchens and pile sheet pans in the center, put plates on the left of the work table, and salad in front. One person could place the plates on a tray, put the salad on, and turn and slide the tray onto the cart. This way one person could pre-plate all the salads for our banquet.

Use Bins or Fixtures

This reduces the effort expended by the worker by placing the supplies where they are readily accessible. They have done away with the best example I have ever had of this. When Steak and Shake was at the height of its effort in food service, it had a person who worked the carryout or curb service window. Everything was in little bins right above the window and the person just stood there and never moved. Everything was pre-positioned for them.

In our kitchen at school we use portable and mobile bins to bring the product to the person doing the work rather than making the person go to the product.

Use Motions with the Least Body Movement Wherever Possible

This is laying out a table or a working area confined to the lowest classification of movement that is possible. Use only fingers and wrists or fingers and forearms so that you can work with the least effort expended.

Work with Both Hands

There should be a balance between your hands so that they start and end each motion at the same time. This is simply to build up a smooth operating technique. Somebody told me that you should hire people who are bright, but lazy, because they are going to find an easier way to do things. If you hire someone who is energetic, but stupid, they will work themselves to death. You must always be looking for an easier way to do it. That is what this system with Gilbreth is about. The story of Gilbreth was "Cheaper by the Dozen," an old movie with Clifton Webb and Myrna Loy who were raising 12 children. Everything in the house was based on an efficient method of operation for rearing these 12 children. As a father, Gilbreth would even use a stop watch to time the children's baths. Let's look for an easier and better way of doing our work. We have not done much of this engineering in what we do.

Use Drop Delivery

Whenever possible, work so that you release the product and do not have to pick it up. Have you seen someone who's job was to chop onions in the kitchen. They then try to pick all these chopped onions up and put them into a pan. If they would turn the knife over, put the pan under the chopping board, and simply push them off, it would be much more efficient. Drop things into a chute or conveyer to dispose them while handling then as little as possible.

Use Good Posture and Sight

Whenever possible, allow the worker to vary his position to either sitting or standing, but try and arrange it so he doesn't have to strain to see. Make sure the posture is right for the employee. At one of the first operations where I worked, we had a lady who worked for us who was a pot and pan washer. She was one of the tiniest people you have ever seen in your life. I do not know if you have ever seen a tiny, short person try and get into a pot and pan sink, but it is really difficult. This woman had to stand on two Coke cases to get into the sink. By and large, the equipment that we operate and use is not built for females. It is usually the wrong height. This woman standing on two Coke cases was probably not a good safety practice, but it was sure easier for her to get into that pot sink than standing on the floor.

Minimize the Holding by Any One Hand

We frequently find that you stand and one hand does nothing. Try and work in a sequence with both hands. You may do this by introducing fixtures to hold things.

As you look to improve the physical factors, eight questions you could ask or observations that you could make are: (1) Is the work arranged to the best advantage?; (2) Are the tools and materials pre-positioned? Find out what tools they use, when they use the tools, and what procedures they do; (3) Can bins or fixtures ever be used?; (4) Is the work performed being performed with the fewest body movements possible?; (5) Is there a rhythm to the procedure they are doing?; (6) Can drop delivery be used?; (7) Are the conditions of posture and sight as good as can be provided?; and (8) Is the work being held by either hand in the process of doing?

SALES MONITORING

The food service manager prepares a forecast of business for each day. Then the manager will calculate the number of people needed to fill the production or service requirement. One way that is used to judge the ability of employees is to calculate sales per worker. This is total sales divided by the number of workers. If the salads produced bring $500, then that divided by 2 would be $250 in sales per worker. We use this as a basis to judge management efficiency and effectiveness in the industry.

Another ratio we use is wages per worker. Divide your sales by the cost of labor. Sales are $22,218,547. Your cost of labor is $5,394,055. This would indicate that for every $4.12 of sales you are required to spend $1 in labor cost. If we estimate our volume is

Labor Control 8-15

going to be $500 for Friday night, we can divide that by our cost of labor factor, and know that for every $4.12 in sales, we are going to spend $1 in labor for the volume we do.

Establish a budget for labor and make the comparison of actual to forecast and we can determine if we are over or under budget on payroll.

If you work in retailing, at the end of the day, the one question that the supervisor asks is, "Did you make your day?" What this means is how did your sales volume compare to a year ago (the same day, not date, but the same day)? Because of fluctuating holidays and weekends it does not matter about the date, it is the day of a year ago. Always compare sales day to sales day after a year. We start with the number of meals on last year's comparable day.

Consider any unusual circumstances that may have happened either to add to or take away from business on that day. Sometimes they forecast bad weather and snow and then it does not come. This plays havoc with trying to figure out a customer count. Unusual weather will normally have an effect on the volume of business.

Table 8.5 shows a Labor Analysis with the positions, and then an actual over or under figure, comparing what you have budgeted with what you actually used.

Table 8.5 Labor Analysis

Date:	Sales: Forecast $3,000		Actual $2,7000		
	Labor		Labor %		Over/
Employee	Budget	Actual	Budget	Actual	Under
Kitchen	$300.00	$292.50	10%	10.8%	.8%
Cooks	150.00	150.00	5%	5.5%	.5%
Other Kitchen	112.50	105.00	3.75%	3.88%	.13%
Dishwashers	37.50	37.50	1.25%	1.38%	.13%
Dining Room	187.50	177.50	6.25%	6.57%	.32%
Waitress	112.50	107.50	3.75%	3.98%	.23%
Bus People	75.00	70.00	2.5%	2.59%	.09%
TOTAL	$487.50	470.00			

Budget %: 16.2% Actual %: 17.4%
Budget Sales: $6.15 Actual: 5.74
per Labor $

These are considerations we suggest in monitoring the hours that you schedule:

1. What were the actual hours used?
2. What should or could the hours have been?
3. What was the reason for the difference? There may be justifiable reasons, but if there is a deviation you should know why.
4. What changes are necessary to have actual meet budget?

IMPROVEMENT PROCEDURES

The problems you may have are any of the following.

1. An inaccurate forecast of business.—Sometimes we tend to overstaff and do so because if we do not have someone there to do it, who is going to do it?
2. An unrealistic manpower guideline—This is one where we really do not know what the standards or requirements are for a fair day's work.
3. Non-compliance with the guidelines established.—In other words, we set up the guidelines of what to do but when we begin to schedule people, we do not use them.
4. Unpredictable or excessive fluctuations in business volume.—Have you ever worked anywhere where you could not set up a trend of business? I ran one operation where I could never set a pattern of business or forecast accurately. It was incredibly bad. There are some operations that just will not set a pattern.

When you do staffing charts, watch the distribution of the work load and the work productivity per employee at various stations and meal periods. Try and set an even distribution of the work load with the people to cover what needs to be done.

Remedial Measures for Excessive Labor

Review Hours of Operation

You may have no control over hours of operation because many times you are told what hours you are going to operate. Four or five years ago a corporation told every member of its chain in the United States it should stay open 24 hours a day. If this is what was said, it does not matter if a restaurant was busy or not busy; even if it did not serve anybody at night, it stayed open 24 hours. It had no choice on hours of operation. Luckily, most of us have a choice and we may need to take a hard look at the hours of operation we are going to have.

The Use of Relief Schedules

This means days or hours off. Look at the scheduling and a suitable work schedule.

Revision of the Facilities

It could be that you simply cannot afford to revise these facilities but you may find who is using what in a certain area of the kitchen and relocate by making equipment mobile. Put the equipment where the people are to prevent them from having to walk around to get to it.

The following are considerations in establishing staffing charts or guides:

1. Local labor market. The number of people available to work is going to reflect on how you treat people. If you cannot get anyone to work, people may try to get away with lower standards because they know you cannot get anyone else.

2. Training programs. Some people use the magic apron training program. That is, I give you a cook's apron, you put it on, and you are trained. We said there are three things that had to do with labor control—good management, training, and effective scheduling.

3. Layout and design of the area.

4. Equipment. If there is labor-saving equipment (new good equipment) the work is easier. If it is broken and in poor condition the work will take longer.

5. The menu.

6. Type of service. We are beginning to transfer everything to the customer to eliminate labor.

7. Employee morale and motivation. If morale is bad, and there is no motivation, productivity will be poor. You will need to allow for this in scheduling people to work.

8. Raw to ready scale of product. Convenient or ready prepared types of food that may be on the menu will increase productivity.

9. Daily business cycle. Both by days of the week and hours of the open schedule.

Another thing dealing with improvement is incentives for employees to aid in increasing productivity: "If you sell a certain amount, you receive a reward." Some employers give incentives for perfect safety or no accidents over certain periods of time. All of the costs incurred by an employer is predicated on the amount of times the employer must file against workmen's compensation or insurance. If you can effectively reduce the number of accidents in an organization, you effectively reduce the cost of fringes to employees based on insurance or workmen's compensation premiums.

I spent a brief period of time working for a chemical company. At the chemical company, the safety program was a major consideration within that company because when there are accidents at a chemical company they do not mean just cutting a finger—they mean blowing up people or a whole city. If an employee went so many months or a year without what they call a lost time accident, all the employees were very handsomely rewarded on the safety program, which is a means of reducing the cost of labor.

An important element to remember with employee incentives is that they must be something that will motivate that employee. Some incentives that have been successfully used are things like a better shift, more overtime, less overtime and requested days off, a greater opportunity to earn bonus points or customer tips, better locker space, or even a special place to park. You may want to consider letting the employee choose from a group of possible rewards for meeting certain standards of work performance.

Summary

The cost of labor is one of a number of problems we must deal with as we operate our restaurants. Our ability to train our people influences our ability to control our labor costs. Controlling labor involves forecasting, scheduling, monitoring, and improving. Develop a method of forecasting business that reflects your operation and then develop a system of scheduling people for your operation. Some of the things you may want to consider in developing your own system of scheduling are: labor cost percentages by department; units of output per employee; use of a Gantt Chart to illustrate who, what, and when; employee productivity; and work load distribution. You must have some method of evaluating your schedule system and know how to make changes in your operation. Some of the things that are to be considered when improvement is needed are: the physical factors of your work areas and the principles of motion economy.

Sales are the way we measure success or failure of our business. By relating labor costs to our volume of business, we have a logical way of looking at how well we are using the labor that is available to us. Several ratios can be used. Use the one that makes most sense to you. Take into consideration all the elements that affect how well your people are able to perform and try to improve in the areas that will give you the best return.

Form 8.1
GANTT CHART

Meal: _____   Date: _____

Employee	10:00	10:30	11:00	11:30	12:00	12:30	1:00	1:30	2:00

Labor Control

Form 8.2
GANTT CHART

Meal: _____ Date: _____

Employee	7:00	8:00	9:00	10:00	11:00	12:00	1:00	2:00	3:00

Form 8.3
GANTT CHART

Meal: _____   Date: _____

Employee	7:00	8:00	9:00	10:00	11:00	12:00	1:00	2:00	3:00
A.M. Kitchen Supv.	Check Inventory Menu Schedules	Receive Deliveries	Call in Orders	Dining Room Meeting	Coordinate	Solve Problems	Kitchen Meeting	Purchase Order Lunch Break	Records
Line Cook	Setup Station Start Sauces	Sauce Prep Trim & Portion Meat	Roast Meat	Break Setup Line	Work Line	Work Line	Work Line Kitchen Meeting	Lunch Break Store Food	
Back-Up Cook		Setup Station Clean Veg	Trim & Portion Veg Prep Soup	Setup Line	Break Work Line	Work Line	Work Line	Lunch Break	
Pantry		Setup Station Wash Lettuce	Wash Spinach Prep Dressing	Setup Salads Setup Line Break	Make Sandwiches	Work Line	Work Line Kitchen Meeting		
Steward	Clean Storeroom	Store Deliveries	Fill Requisitions Setup Pot Sink	Wash Pots Empty Trash Store Deliveries	Break Wash Pots	Help Where Needed	Empty Trash Lunch Break	Mop Kitchen Clean Trash Area	
Dishroom				Setup Dish Machine	Help Where Needed Wash Dishes	Wash Dishes	Store Dishes		
Dishroom				Help with Pots Wash Dishes	Wash Dishes Run Dishes		Wash & Store Dishes		

Chapter 9

Training Evaluation

About every six months or so, I go to my doctor for a check up. He looks into my eyes, listens to my heart and lungs, bangs on my knees and elbows with his little hammer, and watches how I walk. He writes down his observations on my file and then, after I get myself back together, we talk about my condition. We talk about anything out of the ordinary in the past and we look at what is coming up in the future. Sometimes, we just keep things the way they are, but other times he may change my prescription. Even if it seems like we are not doing anything special, I still keep my appointment every six months or so.

The evaluation of your training program ought to be like this. Every six months or so you want to check up on how it is doing. Regular evaluation lets people know the training program is important to management. Training needs change, better methods or material may become available, different people may take on the duties of training, and the trainees change. You want to look at the program objectively, keep what is working well, and make adjustments where things have changed.

EVALUATION FACTORS

There are certain signs you look for to see if your training program is healthy. Let's look at some of the symptoms that provide evidence about the effectiveness of a human resources development program:

Employee tenure.
Absenteeism.

Injury and illness.
Turnover rates.
Workers' skill level.

Employee Tenure

How many months and how many years have employees stayed with you? This is an easy thing to check. If people are staying with you, it is a good sign they feel competent in their jobs. Length of service, though, is not the only thing tc consider. What is their interest level in the organization and how well do they cooperate with you and with other workers? The following is a checklist that will help you analyze the strength of an employee's tenure (Checklist 9.1).

Many employees are afraid to take risks or try to solve problems for fear of making a mistake. Mistakes are great learning devices, provided they are used as a way to teach a better way of solving a problem as opposed to an unsatisfactory performance evaluation. Making a mistake and learning from it is a source of development. If your training program uses mistakes as an opportunity to improve skills and not a way to put down a new person, employees will be more open and honest about how they feel about their job. Your ability to know about problems has a great deal to do with your ability to solve problems. A stronger more open relationship develops when people think you care about their work-related problems and will try to solve them.

Absenteeism

Most people who work in human resource management feel the reasons why employees do not come to work are predictable. If you are showing high absenteeism, it could be due to management insensitivity to some critical issue for an employee.

It is critical your employees have a sense of self-worth and know they are valuable members of your team. A knowledge of the importance of the job and how each job fits into the operation of the restaurant should be given during the orientation training of the new employee. It is important the orientation to the job stresses the value of the job to the operation so the employee who performs that job well can develop a sense of self-worth.

It is also important to carefully observe the employee during the training and probationary period. If the employee does not develop the skills or show the attitude needed, this is the time to remove them from the payroll. The employee that is careless about showing up for work during the probationary period is not going to

Checklist 9.1

EMPLOYEE TENURE STRENGTH

Weak Link	*Strong Link*
Sees something wrong and does nothing about it.	Feels free to talk about difficulties. Expects problems to be solved.
Leaves management alone. Somehow policies and procedures do not get carried out.	There is a noticeable sense of team play; a sharing of responsibility.
Engages in competition when cooperation is needed.	Easily requests the help of others and is willing to give help.
In a crisis, will withdraw or start blaming someone else.	In a crisis, quickly works with others to solve porblem.
Engages in covert conflicts and plays games or politics.	Considers conflict necessary to decision making and growth. Deals openly and effectively with conflict.
Avoids giving feedback.	Joint critique of progress is routine.
Works to minimize risk.	Accepts risk as a condition of growth and change.
Glosses over poor performance.	Poor performance is jointly resolved.
Swallows frustration: "I can do nothing; it's their' responsibility to save the ship."	Frustrations are the call to action: "It's my responsibility to save the ship."

improve this careless attitude when the probationary period is completed. The longer a person who cannot do the job or will not do the job works for you, the greater the damage done to your business.

Illness and Injury

When morale is low on the job, people just do not feel good at work. They feel burned out. They get sick easily and miss a lot of days. With poor morale, a job can have so much stress and unhappiness people can develop real illnesses.

A rash of cuts and burns may be a symptom of a morale problem but it may also be a symptom of a training problem. Have the people been taught the details of how to care for a knife? Have they been taught not to pick up hot pans with wet towels? It seems so elementary to use the correct procedure for lifting and carrying but have these procedures been explained in your training program? Strained backs and dropped trays may indicate this has not been taught or learned.

Turnover Rates

If you treat employee mistakes with a positive approach, it will reduce turnover rates and lower costs. A punitive approach raises costs by increasing turnover. The biggest problem of using the positive approach is in shifting from one approach to the other. It is hard to begin to teach, to help, or to develop someone who makes mistakes when you have always reprimanded, warned, threatened, and punished.

A turnover rate is calculated by dividing the number of people hired within a certain time period by the total number of jobs in an operation. If your operation has 20 jobs and you have hired 20 people in the last three months, you have a 100 percent turnover rate for that three-month period. What really happens is there are a couple of jobs that turnover constantly. Those 20 people you hired may have all been hired to be buspeople or dishwashers. If you can develop your patience and insist on a good training period for those buspeople and dishwashers, you can reduce that 100 percent turnover. If you can reduce that 100 percent to 10 percent, doesn't it make sense to improve your training program? It is a lot better to spend your time training two people well than to go through the whole recruiting, hiring, and training process with 20 people. Training will reduce turnover, but do not expect training to eliminate turnover given the uncommitted attitude among many workers in the hospitality industry.

Worker Skill Level

When workers lack skills they should have been trained in, it may indicate that your training procedures were inadequate. Workers you hire who rate poorly in every respect, reflect on your hiring practices. Both inadequate training and inconsistent hiring indicate areas for improvement on your part.

PERFORMANCE APPRAISAL PROGRAM

An important part of a restaurant's marketing image is the service attitude of the employees. You should think of performance appraisal as a marketing function. Marketing involves an awareness of the needs of the customer and an awareness of how well the product or service meets the needs of the customer. You want to appraise performance both through the eyes of the customer and in comparison to your standards of performance.

Customer Appraisal

In reality, the evaluation of your training methods will be performed by your customers. A restaurant is really a reflection of the people who are attracted by your selection of food and beverage products and your method of service. They will vote yes or no on the success of the restaurant.

It is vital to be in constant communication with your customers to find out their likes and dislikes and to answer their questions. Customer contact by management is critical to the image of the restaurant and provides a continuous evaluation of customer acceptance of your products and your service personnel.

How many professionals do you have in your restaurant who will do a sales presentation to the customer when they take the order? How many instead, issue a challenge to the customer, "You don't want dessert, do you?" Or how many comment, "I don't know how it tastes. We don't get to eat that." If you have professionals who are doing sales promotions at the time they take the order, this is indicative of good employee training.

My wife and I once went out for dinner to a rather well-known restaurant in Michigan and asked the waitress what she would recommend from the menu if she were having dinner there. Her immediate response was, "Nothing. I'd have a cheese sandwich; I'm a vegetarian." Such a comment has a tremendously negative effect upon sales (Miller, 1987).

It is difficult for a manager to see all sides of a situation. Personal contact with the customer is important, but there are also other sources of information to find out how the customer feels about you. The customer votes about the best product with the selection of menu items, and keeping track of the sales of each menu item provides you with the answer to what are we doing that they like. The sales history of menu specials that are not written on the menu and are described by the serving staff answers the question who is doing the best job of suggested selling.

Customer comment cards and customer survey cards are other sources of information for the busy manager. Some of the questions you would like to have answered relate to what is unique about us that the customers like or how can we improve to better serve their needs. Keep customer comment cards brief and to the point. You want to make it easy for the customer to express an opinion. Your sales history will tell you which menu items they like. The customer comment cards can tell why they come to your restaurant or maybe why they have a poor experience. Form 9.1 shows two customer comment cards. As you can see, they make it very easy for the customer to express an opinion. If they do put their name and address on the comments, a personal letter of response and a thank you for the comments should be sent.

Form 9.2 is a copy of a form for a shopper's critique. This is one page of a six-page report that is completed for each area of the restaurant, bar, host or hostess, dining room, waiter/waitress, table set-up, food, restrooms, and additional comments. As you can see from Form 9.3, the shopper's report revealed significant deficiencies in performance.

All of your sources of information about the customer are gathered to help you see the restaurant through the eyes of the customer. What does the customer see, what does the customer feel, and what is the image of the restaurant in the customer's eyes? Focusing on your restaurant through the eyes of the customer will help you envision what is right and what could be better.

Employee Performance Review

A performance review is a tool to be used as part of a general evaluation of human resources. A responsibility of management is a regular evaluation of employee performance. There are several parts to an evaluation system: informing the employee about the performance review process, documenting and talking to employees twice a month on performance, preparing for a six-month performance review, completing the form, talking to the employee about performance and goal achievement, and setting goals for the next work period.

Performance reviews can be explained during the orientation process. While the worker is being trained, it can be pointed out they will be evaluated during the performance review on what they are being trained to do. You may show the evaluation form to the new employee during training to reinforce the value of the training. People should know in advance when the performance review will take place, the basis for the evaluation and should feel it will be fair.

You want to talk to your employees on a regular basis about their performance. On your schedule of daily activities, make a list of three or four employees that you will observe that day. A Five-Minute Evaluation form can be used to discuss your observations with the employee. Form 9.4 is a form from a seminar, "The Labor Issue: Hiring, Training, and Retaining," presented by Jeffery Harrison with the Educational Foundation of the National Restaurant Association. What you want is a simple form that allows you to document performance on a regular basis. This particular form gives you a basis for talking to the employee and having the employee give feedback about the job without taking a lot of time.

Prior to making the six-month employee performance review, prepare yourself by reviewing the job description, the individual goals set by the employee, and the Five-Minute Evaluation forms. Set up a system so you know which employees are due for a review each month.

The procedure for making a performance review usually requires a form. The form will list the performance categories and specify some sort of a rating system. Most forms include: the quality of job performance; work habits; attendance; appearance; how the worker relates to peers, supervisors, and customers; and the ability and attitude toward the job. As an example of a performance review form, Form 9.5 is a form from the Labor Issue seminar. In addition to space for assigning a point score for qualities, there is a page that emphasizes goal setting.

Evaluation forms should achieve a balance between too much detail and not enough. You want a form that is simple, yet sets standards and requires a fair amount of thought. Whatever the format, its usefulness depends on how carefully it is filled out. It should be completed thoughtfully and honestly for each person. Evaluate performance rather than personality and be as objective as you can be.

Sharing the results of the evaluation with the employee is another form of communication about the work to be performed. The best way to handle this process is to talk in terms of the work, not the person. It should be a cooperative, problem-solving, two-way discussion that praises good performance and treats improvement as a mutually important goal. Although you may have negative things to report, you can address them as things that can be improved in the future. It should look backward at what has been achieved and forward to further growth development.

The performance review should be another way of communicating with your people. It should tell the employee how she is doing, pinpoint training needs, provide an assessment of hiring practices and training methods, and allow you to reward the people who have earned a reward.

Summary

Evaluation of employee performance is an ongoing process. Every six months or so you want to step back and objectively look at operations and employee performance. How well employees perform and meet your standards is the ultimate test of all your training efforts. Look at the record of absenteeism, turnover, illness, and injury. Appraise performance of employees both through the eyes of the customer and in comparison to your standards. Personal contact with customers, analysis of menu sales, customer comment cards, and professional shoppers reports provide insight into the customer's view of the restaurant. A performance review with the appropriate forms is the time to see if employees are consistently meeting your standards.

REFERENCES

Forrest, Lewis C., Jr. 1990. *Training for the Hospitality Industry.* East Lansing, MI: Educational Institute of the American Hotel and Motel Association, pp. 241-264. This is a chapter on evaluating training programs.

Harrison, Jeffery A. 1990. *The Labor Issue: Hiring, Training and Retaining.* Chicago: The Education Foundation of the National Restaurant Association, pp. 123-128. This is the resource book that is used for the seminar.

Martin, Robert J. 1986. *Professional Management of Housekeeping Operations.* New York: John Wiley and Sons, Inc., pp 265-270. This is a discussion of performance appraisals in a chapter on subroutines.

Miller, Jack E. 1987. *Menu Pricing and Strategy.* New York: Van Nostrand Reinhold, Co., pp. 50, 51.

Miller, Jack E. and Mary Porter. 1985. *Supervision in the Hospitality Industry.* New York: John Wiley and Sons, Inc., pp. 171-192. This is a chapter on Evaluating Performance.

Training Evaluation

Form 9.1

COMMENT CARD

PLEASE

In order that we may give you the best possible service, we would appreciate it if you would let us know if there is anything about our food or service that does not entirely please you. Further, should you receive a steak that is not cooked to your satisfaction or if the food is not hot, please let your waitress or the Maitre d' know immediately.

Your Waitress is _____ Table Number _____

Special Remarks: _____
_____
_____
_____

You may drop this card in the box by the front door or in the mail.

Name _____

Address _____ Phone _____

WE ARE CONTINUALLY TRYING TO IMPROVE OUR SERVICE ON THE "SPIRIT" OF ST. CHARLES. YOUR COMMENTS ARE APPRECIATED.

	EXCELLENT	GOOD	FAIR	POOR
ENTERTAINMENT	☐	☐	☐	☐
FOOD	☐	☐	☐	☐
SERVICE	☐	☐	☐	☐

HOW DID YOU HEAR ABOUT THE "SPIRIT" _____
_____
_____

ADDITIONAL COMMENTS _____
_____
_____
_____

Form 9.2

COMMENT SHEET

IV. **Waiter / Waitress:**

    Name or No.:   **Identification:**

    Dress and Personal Grooming:

    Suggestive Salesmanship:

    Greeting and Farewell:

    Requests for additional food or service and check back:

    Service Comments:

    Time and Service:

        Order repeated to guest:
        Noticeable delay in service:
        Food served as ordered:
        Dessert order taken and served promptly:

    Check:

        Correctly priced:
        Correctly totaled:
        Legible:

Training Evaluation

Form 9.3

COMMENT SHEET

IV. **Waiter / Waitress:**

Name or No.:
No name tag
Could not read check

Identification:
5'3" - 130 lbs. Dark hair
Seated at 4 top on south wall table.

Dress and Personal Grooming:
Apron was soiled. She was not wearing a name tag.

Suggestive Salesmanship:
None. Requested dessert and more coffee.

Greeting and Farewell:
None. Approached table and waited for the order to be given.

Requests for additional food or service and check back:
No check back during the meal.

Service Comments:
Served the dessert but did not bring forks with dessert—had to make second trip with the forks. Waitress placed order between guests at the counter, then came around counter, picked up order, and served to table next to ours.

Time and Service:
    Order repeat to guest: No
    Noticeable delay in service: No
    Food served as ordered: Yes
    Dessert order taken and served promptly: Had to gain the attention of the waitress to give our dessert order.

Check:
    Correctly priced: No. (Club Sand. was not charged.)
    Correctly totaled: Yes
    Legible: Yes (except for waitress name or number).

Form 9.4

FIVE-MINUTE EVALUATION

> **Date:** _____
>
> **Name:** _____
>
> **Area Working:** _____
>
> **Manager:** _____
>
> **Reinforcement Feedback**
>
> 1. Work Place: _____
>
> 2. Teamwork: _____
>
> 3. Guest Focus: _____
>
> **Positive Feedback**
>
> 1. Work Place: _____
>
> 2. Teamwork: _____
>
> 3. Guest Focus: _____
>
> 4. Thanks for the Help: _____
>
> Employee Feedback to Management: _____
>
> Gameplan: _____
>
> Meet Next Time: _____
>
> Employee Signature: _____
>
> Manager Signature: _____
>
> Date: _____
>
> File Date: _____

Source: Jeffery Harrison

Form 9.5

EMPLOYEE PERFORMANCE REVIEW

Date: _____
Unit: _____

Employee Name: _____ Manager's Name: _____
Position: _____

Purpose of Review:
- ☐ Six Month Review
- ☐ Position Change
- ☐ Transfer
- ☐ Promotion
- ☐ Other _____

	1 Superior	2 Above Average	3 Satisfactory	4 Needs Improvement	5 Unsatisfactory	6 Not Applicable
I. Attendance						
A. Punctuality						
B. Days Missed						
C. Proper Notification						
II. Personal Qualifications						
A. Appearance						
B. Personality						
C. Tact / Courtesy						
III. Ability						
A. Rate of Learning						
B. Initiative						
C. Judgment						
D. Job Knowledge						
E. Follows Instructions						
IV. Attitude Toward Job						
A. Interest						
B. Cooperation						
C. Work Habits						
D. Responsibility / Dependability						
E. Adjustments to Changes						
F. Responsive to Constructive Criticism						
V. Job Performance						
A. Accuracy						
B. Neatness						
C. Productivity						
D. Amount of Supervision Required						
E. Thoroughness						

Form 9.5 (continued)

1. Review of achievements as related to last established goals: _____

2. Goals to be met in future: _____

3. Employee's STRONGEST points: _____

4. Employee's WEAKEST points: _____

5. Advancement capabilities: _____

Employee's remarks: _____

*Employee Signature   Date

*The employee's signature in no way shows that he/she agrees with the evaluation. It merely indicates that the employee has seen the evaluation and understands the contents.

Manager's Signature   Date

Appendix A

State Supervisory Personnel for Marketing Education

ALABAMA

Bob Hollis
   State Department of Education
   State Office Building, Room 823
   Montgomery, AL 36130
   (205) 261-5189

Ann West
   Route 3, Box 68
   Haleyville, AL 35565

ALASKA

Linda E. Van Ballenberghe
   Alaska Department of Education
   Post Office Box F
   Juneau, AK 99811
   (907) 465-4685

ARIZONA

Dave Muehlbauer
   Arizona Department of Education
   1535 West Jefferson Street
   Phoenix, AZ 85007
   (602) 255-5354

Cathy Shadle
   (same as above)
   (602) 255-5197

ARKANSAS

Ms. Tommie Butler
   Department of Education
   #3 Capitol Mall
   Luther S. Hardin Building,
   Room 305-D
   Little Rock, AR 72201
   (501) 682-1768

Bill Robinson
   (same as above)

Ms. Kay Baker
   (same as above)

Richard Mahan
   (same as above)

Ms. Hettie Lou Martin
   (same as above)

CALIFORNIA

Gary E. Thompson (Secondary)
   State Department of Education
   721 Capitol Mall
   Sacramento, CA 95814
   (916) 445-5182

Douglas D. Mahr
   (same as above)
   (916) 445-5183

Carroll Bravo
   (same as above)
   (916) 445-8882

Lee Murdock
   1919 21st Street
   Sacramento, CA 95814

Charles Brown
   1111 Jackson St., Room 4075
   Oakland, CA 94607

Bernard Norton
   (same as above)

Marty Hays
　California State Polytechnic University
　Business Education Center
　School of Business
　3801 West Temple Avenue
　Pomona, CA 91768

Rebecca Singleton (Postsecondary)
　Chancellor's Office
　California Community Colleges
　1107 9th Street
　Sacramento, CA 95814
　(916) 445-0486

COLORADO

Mrs. Diane Hegeman
　Colorado Community College and

Occupational Education System
　1391 North Speer Boulevard, Suite 600
　Denver, CO 80204-2554
　(303) 620-4000

CONNECTICUT

Ronald J. DeGregory
　State Department of Education
　Division of Vocational, Technical and

Adult Education
　25 Industrial Park Road
　Middletown, CT 06457
　(203) 638-4056

Ronald A. Stancil
　(same as above)
　(203) 638-4065

DELAWARE

John G. Townsend Building
　State Department of Public Instruction
　Post Office Box 1402
　Dover, DE 19903
　(302) 736-4681

DISTRICT OF COLUMBIA

Mrs. Nina L. Gaskin
　Browne Supervisory Unit
　Division of Career and Adult
　Education
　26th Street and Benning Road, N.E.
　Washington, DC 20002
　(202) 724-3916

FLORIDA

John E. Frazier
　Department of Education
　Knott Building
　Tallahassee, FL 32399
　(904) 488-0482

Douglas T. Johnson
　(same as above)

Loretta Cordell
　(same as above)

Michael F. Cahill
　400 W. Robinson St., Suite 602
　Orlando, FL 32801

GEORGIA

Marvin M. Brown
　Division of Secondary Programs
　Office of Vocational Education
　1770 Twin Towers East
　Atlanta, GA 30334-5040
　(404) 656-2541

Joyce Mauldin
　(same as above)

GUAM

Russell Tufvander
　(DECA, Inc. Representative)
　GCC
　High School Division
　Box 23069
　Main Postal Facility
　Agana, GU 96921

HAWAII

Mr. Yukio Toyama
　Occupational Development Section
　941 Hind Iuka Drive

Appendix A

Honolulu, HI 96821
(808) 373-3356

IDAHO

Bruce Albright
State Board of Vocational Education
Len B. Jordan Building
650 West State Street
Boise, ID 83720
(208) 334-2659

ILLINOIS

Mrs. Gerry B. Gaedtka
100 North First Street
Springfield, IL 62777
(217) 782-4877

Roger Uhe
(same as above)

INDIANA

Steve Darnell
Indiana Department of Education
Center for School Improvement
Vocational Education Section
State House, Room 229
Indianapolis, IN 46204-2798
(317) 232-9184

Philip E. Myers
(same as above)

IOWA

Jayne A. Sullivan (Secondary)
Bureau of Career Education
Department of Education
Grimes State Office Building
Des Moines, IA 50319
(515) 281-8488

Donald G. Smith (Postsecondary)
Bureau of Area Schools
Department of Education
Grimes State Office Building
Des Moines, IA 50319
(515) 281-4723

KANSAS

Richard Russell
Vocational Education
Kansas State Department of Education
120 East 10th Street
Topeka, KS 66612
(913) 296-4921

Karen Kirk
State DECA Sponsor
Family Center, Box 4
Emporia State University
Emporia, KS 66801
(316) 343-1200 Ext. 5430

KENTUCKY

William T. Jeffrey
Office of Vocational Education
2112 Capitol Plaza Tower
Frankfort, KY 40601
(502) 564-3775

Gary Colvin
State DECA Advisor
(same as above)

LOUISIANA

Carol Lynn Borskey
State Department of Education
Post Office Box 94064
Capitol Station
Baton Rouge, LA 70804-9064
(504) 342-3445

MAINE

Maurice Parent
Bureau of Vocational Education
Department of Educational and
Cultural Services
State House Station 23
Augusta, ME 04333
(207) 289-5854

MARYLAND

Richard C. Kiley

Division of Vocational Education
State Department of Education
200 West Baltimore Street
Baltimore, MD 21201
(301) 333-2083

MASSACHUSETTS

Elaine Cadigan
  Bureau of Program Services
  Division of Occupational Education
  1385 Hancock Street
  Quincy, MA 02169
  (617) 770-7354

Elena Swaim
  (same as above)
  (617) 770-7365

MICHIGAN

Tom Benton
  Vocational-Technical Education Service
  Michigan Department of Education
  Post Office Box 30009
  Lansing, MI 48909
  (417) 335-0381

David G. Wait
  DECA Project Consultant
  204 B Sill Hall
  Eastern Michigan University
  Ypsilanti, MI 48197
  (313) 487-0133

MINNESOTA

Patrick E. DiPlacido
  Secondary Vocational Education
  Department of Education
  624 Capitol Square Building
  550 Cedar Street
  St. Paul, MN 55101
  (612) 296-3306

Lynda Rago (Postsecondary)
  State Board of Vocational Technical Education
  Instructional Services Section
  Capitol Square Building
  550 Cedar Street
  St. Paul, MN 55101
  (612) 297-1484

MISSISSIPPI

James Bowers
  State Department of Education
  Vocational Education Division
  Post Office Box 771
  Jackson, MS 39205
  (601) 359-3465

Gregg Sheffield
  (same as above)

MISSOURI

Dr. Gene Reed
  Department of Elementary and Secondary Education
  Post Office Box 480
  Jefferson Building
  Jefferson City, MO 65101
  (314) 751-4367

Linda Turner
  (same as above)

MONTANA

Roger Swearengen
  Office of Public Instruction
  State Capitol
  Helena, MT 59620
  (406) 444-4556

NEBRASKA

Gregg Christensen
  Division of Vocational Education
  301 Centennial Mall South
  Post Office Box 94987
  Lincoln, NE
  (402) 471-4803

Richard Campbell
  (same as above)
  (401) 471-4808

Appendix A

NEVADA

Evelyn Miller
  Occupational Education
  Department of Education
  Capitol Complex
  Carson City, NV 89710
  (702) 885-3144

NEW HAMPSHIRE

James C. Stopa
  Division of Instructional Services
  Bureau of Vocational-Technical
  Education
  Department of Education
  State Office Park South
  101 Pleasant Street
  Concord, NH 03301
  (603) 271-3186

NEW JERSEY

Chuck Coligan
  Division of Vocational Education
  Department of Education
  225 West State Street, CN 500
  Trenton, NJ 08625
  (609) 292-6575

NEW MEXICO

Darrell Jones
  Department of Education
  Education Building
  Santa Fe, NM 87501
  (505) 827-6646

NEW YORK

Robert Jaffarian
  Bureau of Business and Health
  Occupations
  New York State Education Department
  One Commerce Plaza, Room 1615
  Albany, NY 12234
  (518) 474-6240 or 486-4763

Robert Brennan
  (same as above)

Jon Greenwalt
  (same as above)

Anthony Schilling
  (same as above)

Suzanne Strauss
  (same as above)

NORTH CAROLINA

Horace C. Robertson (Secondary)
  Division of Vocational Education
  Department of Public Instruction
  Education Building
  116 West Edenton Street
  Raleigh, NC 27603-1712
  (919) 733-3186

Becky Watkins
  (same as above)

Dan Greaven
  (same as above)

Claudette Bowens (Postsecondary)
  Business Occupations
  Department of Community Colleges
  200 West Jones Street
  Raleigh, NC 27603-1337
  (919) 733-7051

NORTH DAKOTA

Leonard F. Pokladnik
  State Board for Vocational Education
  Capitol Building, 15th Floor
  Bismarck, ND 58505
  (701) 224-3182

OHIO

Dr. Larry Casterline
  Division of Vocational Education
  Ohio Departments Building
  65 South Front Street
  Columbus, OH 43266-0308
  (614) 466-3891

Philip DeVeny
  (same as above)

Jack Lenz
(same as above)

James Price
(same as above)

LaVerne Dillon
(same as above)

Carl Kemery
(same as above)

Rick Mangini
(same as above)

Dee Sturgill
Vocational Instructional Materials Laboratory
Student Services Building
154 West 12th Avenue
The Ohio State University
Columbus, OH 43210
(614) 292-5001

OKLAHOMA

D. Gene Warner
State Department of Vocational and Technical Education
1500 West Seventh Avenue
Stillwater, OK 74074
(405) 377-2000 Ext. 244

Robert A. Foley
(same as above)

OREGON

Fay E. Jensen
Oregon Department of Education
700 Pringle Parkway, S.E.
Salem, OR 97310
(503) 378-3590

PENNSYLVANIA

E. H. Blyler
Department of Education
333 Market Street
Harrisburg, PA 17126-0333
(717) 783-8506

PUERTO RICO

Mrs. Carmen H. Perez
Division of Vocational and Technical Education
Department of Education
Box 759
Hato Rey, PR 00919
(809) 754-1295

Mrs. Carmen Doris Diaz Arroyo
(same as above)

Ms. Maria G. Hernandez Umpierre
(same as above)

Mrs. Maria I. Rivera Estrada
(same as above)

RHODE ISLAND

Robert N. Forest
Department of Education
Roger Williams Building
Hayes Street
Providence, RI 02908
(401) 277-2691

SOUTH CAROLINA

Mrs. Ellen C. Vaughan
Office of Vocational Education
State Department of Education
900 Rutledge Building
Columbia, SC 29201
(803) 734-8411

SOUTH DAKOTA

Paula Hess
Office of Vocational Education
Richard F. Kneip Building
700 Governors Drive
Pierre, SD 57501-2293
(605) 773-3247

TENNESSEE

Melissa O. Wilson
Division of Vocational Technical Education

Appendix A

213 Cordell Hull Building
Nashville, TN 37219
(615) 741-1931

TEXAS

Berry Sullivan (Secondary)
Texas Education Agency
1701 North Congress Street
Austin, TX 78701
(512) 463-9443

Emmett Eary
(same as above)

Ward McCain
(same as above)

Dr. Robert W. Day (Postsecondary)
Division of Community Colleges and
Technical Institutes
Coordinating Board
Texas College and University System
Post Office Box 12788, Capitol Station
Austin, TX 78711
(512) 462-6300

UTAH

Dale M. Stephens
Utah State Office of Education
250 East 500 South
Salt Lake City, UT 84111
(801) 533-5574

VERMONT

Richard Oates
Division of Vocational-Technical
Education
State Department of Education
Montpelier, VT 05602
(802) 828-3101

VIRGINIA

James A. Gray, Jr.
State Department of Education
Post Office Box 60
Richmond, VA 23216
(804) 225-2712

I. W. Baughman
Commonwealth Building, Suite 222
210 Church Avenue, S. W.
Roanoke, VA 24011

W. Elwood Roche
Post Office Box 62
Bridgewater, VA 22812

Dianne Tremblay
DECA Specialist
2015 Westwood Ave., 2nd Floor
Richmond, VA 23230

VIRGIN ISLANDS

Ms. Merle Charles
Business Education
Department of Education
Post Office Box 7224
St. Thomas, VI 00801
(809) 774-3366

WASHINGTON

Jack Ray (Secondary)
Division of Vocational-Technical and
Adult Education Services
Office of Superintendent of Public
Instruction
Old Capitol Building
Mail Stop FG-11
Olympia, WA 98504
(206) 753-2060

Dr. Patricia Green (Postsecondary)
State Board for Community College
Education
319 7th Avenue
Olympia, WA 98504-3111
(206) 753-3662

Ken Owen
Vocational Student Organizations
(same as above)

WEST VIRGINIA

Gene Coulson
Bureau of Vocational, Technical and
Adult Education

Capitol Complex
Building No. 6, Room B-243
1900 Washington Street East
Charleston, WV 25305
(304) 348-3896

WISCONSIN

Marie J. Burbach (Secondary)
State Department of Public Instruction
125 South Webster
Post Office Box 7841
Madison, WI 53707
(608) 267-9253

David Hague (Postsecondary)
Wisconsin Board of Vocational,
Technical and Adult Education
310 Price Place
Post Office Box 7874
Madison, WI 53707
(608) 266-1599

WYOMING

State Department of Education
Hathaway Building
Cheyenne, WY 82002
(307) 777-6243

PUBLICATIONS

Culinary and Hospitality Industry
Publications Service (C.H.I.P.S.)
1307 Golden Bear Lane
Kingwood, TX 77339
Fax (713) 359-2277
Telephone (713) 359-2270

Delmar Publishers, Inc.
2 Computer Drive, West
Albany, NY 12214-5511
Telephone (800) 347-7707

Ecolab
Institutional Products Division
Ecolab Center
St. Paul, MN 55102

Educational Institute
American Hotel and Motel Association
Post Office Box 1240
East Lansing, MI 48826
Fax (517) 353-5527
Telephone (517) 353-5500
(includes videos)

John Wiley and Sons, Inc.
Professional and Trade Division

605 Third Avenue
New York, NY 10158

National Restaurant Association
The Educational Foundation
250 South Wacker Drive, Suite 1400
Chicago, IL 60606
Telephone (312) 715-1010
(includes videos)

National Restaurant Association
Publications Department
1200 Seventeenth Street, N.W.
Washington, DC 20036
Telephone (800) 424-5156
         (202) 331-5900
(includes videos)

Prentice-Hall
Simon and Schuster
Englewood Cliffs, NJ 07632

Van Nostrand Reinhold
115 Fifth Avenue
New York, NY 10003
Telephone (212) 254-3232

VIDEO

Britannica Training and Development
310 South Michigan Avenue
Chicago, IL 60604
Fax (312) 347-7903
Telephone (800) 554-9862

C.H.I.P.S.
1307 Golden Bear Lane
Kingwood, TX 77339
Fax (713) 359-2277
Telephone (713) 359-2270

The Learning Resource Center
The Culinary Institute of America
Hyde Park, NY 12538

National Educational Media, Inc.
(A Britannica Company)
310 South Michigan Avenue
Chicago, IL 60604

Fax (312) 347-7903
Telephone (800) 554-9662

Professional Waiters School
Training Videos
17924 Tarzana Street
Encino, CA 91316
Telephone (818) 996-0404

RMI Media Productions
2807 West 47th Street
Shawnee Mission, KS 66205
Fax (913) 362-6910
Telephone (800) 821-5480

Vocational Media Associates
Box 1050
Mount Kisco, NY 10549-9989
Telephone (800) 431-1242

Appendix B

American Culinary Federation Educational Institute

APPRENTICESHIP PROGRAMS

ALABAMA

ACF Birmingham, Alabama Chapter
 Janie Greene
 Jefferson State Junior College
 2601 Carson Road
 Birmingham, AL 35215
 Work (205) 853-1200

ACF Metro Mobile Chefs Association
 Levi Ezell, CEC, CCE, AAC
 Carver Technical College
 414 Station Street
 Mobile, AL 36603
 Work (205) 473-8692

ACF Greater Montgomery Chapter
 Mary Ann Ward, CEC, CCE
 Trenholm State Technical College
 1225 Air Base Boulevard
 Montgomery, AL 36108
 Work (205) 262-4728
 Home (205) 272-7245

ARIZONA

Chefs Association of Greater Phoenix
 Louis Borochaner, CPC
 The Boulders Resort
 Post Office Box 2090
 Carefree, AZ 85377
 Work (602) 488-9009
 Home (602) 971-8604

Chefs and Cooks of Southern Arizona
 Bob Shell, CWC, CCE
 Santa Rita Education
 10,000 South Wilmot Road
 Tuscon, AZ 85777
 Work (602) 574-0024 Ext. 5351
 Home (602) 327-3594

ARKANSAS

ACF Little Rock, Arkansas Chapter
 James D. Johnson, CWC
 Post Office Box 5571
 Little Rock, AR 72215
 Work (501) 223-3000 Ext. 613
 Home (501) 843-6646

BAHAMAS

Bahamas Culinary Association
 Mrs. Addimae Rolle, CWC
 Bahamas Hotel Training College
 Post Office Box N 4896
 Nassau, BA
 Work (809) 323-5804

CALIFORNIA

Chefs de Cuisine Association of California
 Werner Glur, CEC
 607 South Park View Street
 Los Angeles, CA 90057

Work (213) 612-4752
Office (213) 385-2941

Chefs Association of the Pacific Coast
　Kay Stickney
　Restaurant & Hotel In. Apprentice & Training Program
　1650 South Amphlett Boulevard, Suite 312
　San Mateo, CA 94402
　Work (415) 341-2941

Orange Empire Chefs Association
　Larry Banaires
　1150 Cerritos Avenue
　Anaheim, CA 92802
　Work (714) 778-6600 Ext. 1317

California Capitol Chefs Association
　Jon Greenwalt, CEC, AAC
　5475 Ashby Lane
　Roseville, CA 95661
　Work (916) 381-9693
　Home (916) 791-2554

Chefs Association of Palm Springs
　Richard Friend
　College of the Desert
　43–500 Monterey Avenue
　Palm Desert, CA 92260
　Work (619) 346-8041 Ext. 395

Chefs Association of San Diego
　William Cheeseman
　San Diego Community College District
　3375 Camino Del Rio South/Room 335
　San Diego, CA 92108
　Work (619) 584-6568

ACF Monterey Peninsula Chef Association
　Cynthia M. Kaiser
　24408 Portola Road
　Carmel, CA 93923
　Work (408) 625-3695
　Home (408) 649-2580

Northern California Chefs Association
　Michael Piccinino
　6945 Pine Drive
　Anderson, CA 96007

Work (916) 225-4829
Home (916) 241-6162

Chefs de Cuisine of Greater Bakersfield
　William P. Coyle
　Bakersfield College, Food Service
　1801 Panorama Drive
　Bakersfield, CA 93305
　Work (805) 395-4345

Wine Country Culinary Alliance
　Michael Sollie, CEC
　432 D Alaska Drive
　Petaluma, CA 94952
　Work (707) 765-7154
　Home (707) 778-6386

Southern California Inland Empire Chefs Association
　Abraham Ybarra
　Joan Mayhew Catering
　Orange Show
　San Bernadino, CA 92404
　Work (714) 884-5716

Santa Cruz Chefs Association
　Don Bernardo
　1855 Silvana Lane
　Santa Cruz, CA 95062
　Work (408) 423-2053
　Home (408) 462-5720

ACF Greater East Bay Chapter
　Joe Rodrigues
　ARA Services Pacific Bell
　2600 Camino Ramon
　San Ramon, CA 94583

COLORADO

Colorado Chefs de Cuisine Association
　Michael J. Campe, CEC
　838 Symes Building
　820 16th Street
　Denver, CO 80202
　Work (303) 893-3333 EXt 465
　Office (303) 571-5653

Chefs Association of Pikes Peak
　John La Brec
　424 Colorado

Appendix B

Sugar City, CO 81076
Home (719) 372-6037

DELAWARE

ACF Demarva Peninsula Chapter
Mr. Joseph Heacock, CEC, CCE
Sussex County Vo-Tech Center
Route 9
Georgetown, DE 19942
Work (302) 865-0961

ACF First State Chefs Association
Bill Martin
R. D. 2, Box 78F
Peacedale Road
Landenberg, PA 19250

DISTRICT OF COLUMBIA

ACF Nations Capitol Chefs
Forrest Bell, III
Congressional Country Club
8500 River Road
Bethesda, MD 20817
Work (301) 365-1600

FLORIDA

ACF Greater Jacksonville Chapter
Ms. Carol Reed, CWC
Post Office Box 14844
Jacksonville, FL 32238
Work (904) 269-3600

ACF Central Florida Chapter
Major Jarman, CEC
7007 Sea World Drive
Orlando, FL 32812
Work (407) 351-3600 Ext. 308
Home (407) 345-5191

Disney World
Tim Rosendahl, Culinary Development
Walt Disney World Company
Post Office Box 10,000
Lake Buena Vista, FL 32830-1000
Work (407) 824-5233

Volusia County Chefs and Cooks
Scott M. Hansen, CEC
794 Sweetbriar Drive
Deltona, FL 32725
Work (904) 767-7350
Home (407) 574-3756

ACF Palm Beach County Chefs
Ron Zabkiewicz
513 Reo Drive
Jupiter, FL 33458
Work (407) 369-7000 Ext. 7119

Tampa Bay Chefs Association
George Pastor, CEC, CCE
3010-D West Mason Place
Tampa, FL 33629
Work (813) 253-7316

ACF Greater Ft. Lauderdale Chapter
George C. Dech
220 Southwest 5th Street
Dania, FL 33004
Home (305) 920-3215

ACF Miami, Florida Chapter
Howard Aller
2040 N. E. 182nd Street
N. Miami Beach, FL 33162
Work (305) 944-9024

ACF St. Augustine Chapter
Tack Bower, CEC
Post Office Box 3673
St. Augustine, FL 32085
Work (904) 824-8128

Southwest Florida Chefs Association
Rainer Drygala
423 S. W. 34th Street
Cape Coral, FL 33904
Work (813) 542-1051

Sarasota Bay Chefs Association
Charles Vosbergh, CEC
220 Sandspoint
Longboat Key Club
Longboat Key, FL 33548

ACF Bay Culinarians
Travis Herr, CCE
Gulf Coast Community College
5320 West Highway 98
Panama City, FL 32401

ACF, Inc., Polk County Chapter
  Larry Mattson, CEC,CCE
  Post Office Box 8196
  Lakeland, FL 33802
  Work (813) 422-6402
  Home (813) 855-8914

ACF Gulf to Lakes Chefs Chapter
  Jim Aro
  Post Office Box 1179
  Eustis, FL 32727
  Work (904) 357-8222 Ext. 253

GEORGIA

ACF Inc., Greater Atlanta Chapter
  John Brantley
  Cherokee Country Club
  665 Hightower Trail
  Atlanta, GA 30350
  Work (404) 993-4407

Golden Isles of Georgia Culinary Association
  Franz Buck, CEC
  404 Couper Avenue
  St. Simons Island, GA. 31522
  Work (912) 638-3611

IDAHO

Idaho State Chefs & Culinaries
  John Fisher, CEC
  331 East First
  Meridian, ID 83642
  Work (800) 523-2865
  Home (208) 342-7286

ILLINOIS

ACF Chicago Chefs de Cuisine
  Larry Posen
  3650 North Fremont
  Chicago, IL 60613
  Work (312) 729-3000 Ext. 2585
  Home (312) 975-1085

ACF Chefs de Cuisine/Quad Cities
  Anthony Kowalczyk, CEC, AAC
  Davenport Club
  Work (319) 324-8920
  Home (309) 755-3990

ACF Heart of Illinois Professional Chefs Association
  Jim Whitecotton
  Post Office Box 688
  Peoria, IL 61652
  Work (309) 676-7106

INDIANA

ACF Greater Indianapolis Chapter
  Cullen Simpson
  100 Woodland Lane
  Carmel, IN 46032

ACF Tri-State Chefs Chapter
  Robert Bird
  Vincennes University
  Culinary Arts Department
  Vincennes, IN 47591
  Work (812) 885-5858
  Home (812) 886-6714

KENTUCKY

ACF Bluegrass Chefs Association
  Robert Karisny
  421 Gibson Avenue
  Lexington, KY 40504
  Work (606) 263-6611
  Home (606) 253-1916

LOUISIANA

ACF New Orleans Chapter
  Jane Williams, Director
  Culinary Apprentice Program of Louisiana
  615 City Park Avenue
  New Orleans, LA 70119
  Work (504) 483-4208

ACF Greater Baton Rouge Chapter
  Kevin Diez
  38278 Highway 74
  Gonzales, LA 70130
  Work (504) 673-8801

Appendix B

MAINE

Casco Bay Culinary Association
  Marty O'Shea
  2 Fort Road
  S.M.V.T.I./Culinary Arts Dept.
  South Portland, ME 04106

MARYLAND

Central Maryland Chefs Association
  Ms. Elaine Heilman
  420 Ednor Road
  Silver Springs, MD 20904
  Work (301) 997-4562
  Home (301) 774-3703

MASSACHUSETTS

ACF Cape Cod & The Islands
  Roland Czekelius, CEC, Executive Chef
  Chatham Bars Inn
  Shore Road
  Chatham, MA 02633
  Work (508) 945-0096
  Home (508) 945-0186

Epicurean Club of Boston
  Stephen Hunn, Executive Chef
  Boston Park Plaza Hotel
  50 Park Plaza
  Boston, MA 02117
  Work (617) 426-2000

MICHIGAN

ACF, Michigan Chefs de Cuisine Association
  Kevin Enright, CEC, CCE
  Oakland Community College
  27055 Orchard Lake Road
  Farmington Hills, MI 48018
  Work (313) 471-7500

ACF Capitol Professional Chefs Association
  John Farris
  Lansing Community College
  419 West Capital
  Lansing, MI 48910

ACF of Northwestern Michigan
  Randolph Lawton, CCE
  Food Service and Hospital Management
  Northwestern Michigan College
  Traverse City, MI 49684
  Work (616) 922-1197
  Home (616) 947-9815

MISSOURI

Chefs de Cuisine of St. Louis
  Ralph Wehner, CWC
  362 Novara
  Ballwin, MO 63021
  Home (314) 394-9915

ACF Greater Kansas City Chefs Association
  Patrick Sweeney
  Johnson County Community College
  12345 College at Quivira
  Overland Park, KS 62210
  Work (913) 469-8500 Ext. 3611

MONTANA

Chefs and Cooks of Montana
  Jack Hemsing, CEC
  Billings Petroleum Club
  Box 1957
  Billings, MT 59103
  Work (406) 252-6702
  Home (406) 652-1149

NEBRASKA

ACF, Professional Chefs of Nebraska
  Gerrine Schreck, CEC, CWC
  3250 South 12th, Apt C-9
  Lincoln, NE 68502
  Work (402) 471-3333 Ext. 219
  Home (402) 423-5165

NEVADA

High Sierra Chefs Association
  Mr. George Skivafilakis
  c/o Truckee Meadows Community

College
7000 Dandini Boulevard
Reno, NV 89512
Work (702) 673-7015

NEW HAMPSHIRE

ACF New Hampshire Chapter
Christopher M. Woodward
Post Office Box 751
Intervale, NH 03845
Work (603) 356-6767
Home (603) 356-3151

Professional Chefs of New Hampshire
Raymond A. Roy, CEC
35 Russell Street
Nashua, NH 03845
Work (617) 486-7770
Home (603) 882-9009

ACF Piscatauqua Chapter
Paulino B. Cavan, CEC
939 Ocean Boulevard
Hampton, NH 03842

Greater Northern New Hampshire Chapter
Phil Learned, CEC
The Balsams Resort Hotel
Dixville Notch, NH 03576
Work (603) 255-3400

NEW JERSEY

Professional Chefs of South Jersey
John Carbone, CCE, CEC, AAC
Post Office Box 157
Port Republic, NJ 08241
Work (609) 652-1726
Home (609) 646-4950

NEW MEXICO

ACF Rio Grande Valley Chapter
Doug Dunning, CCE
Albuquerque Tech-Vocational Inst.

525 Buena Vista, S.E.
Albuquerque, NM 87106
Work (505) 848-1442

Northern New Mexico Chefs Association
Lela Cross
Lafonda Hotel
100 East San Francisco
Sante Fe, NM 87504
Work (505) 982-5511

NEW YORK

Capital District Central New York Chapter
Donald R. Sacca, CEC
111 Industrial Park Road, Apt. 3
Troy, NY 12180
Work (518) 449-8090
School (518) 861-6207

Professional Chefs of Western New York
John Brennan, CEC
1423 22nd Street
Niagara Falls, NY 14305
Work (716) 285-3361

Chefs of Westchester & Lwr Ct
Lisa Brefere, CWC
606 Anderson Hill Road
Purchase, NY 10577
Work (914) 684-9618
Home (914) 949-4019

NORTH CAROLINA

ACF, Inc. Charlotte Chapter
Jim Bowen
2415 Roswell Avenue
Charlotte, NC 28209
Work (704) 376-0741 Ext. 34

Triad Professional Chefs Association
Mitchell Mack
Four Seasons Town Centre
3121 High Point Road at I-40

Appendix B

Greensboro, NC 27407
Work (919) 292-9161 Ext. 193

Professional Chefs of the Carolinas
Fredi Morf
1316 Hickory Hollow Lane
Raleigh, NC 27610
Work (919) 839-0691

ACF Outer Banks Culinary Association
Craig Hartman
Post Office Box 1033
Kill Devil Hill, NC 27948
Work (914) 441-6042

OHIO

ACF Cleveland Culinary Association
Kevin Markert, CWC
217 East Street
Fairport Harbor, OH 44077
Work (216) 248-4310
Home (216) 352-3284

ACF Columbus Chefs Chapter
Carol Kizer, CCE
Columbus Technical Institute
550 East Spring Street
Columbus, OH 43215
Work (614) 227-2579
Home (614) 488-8907

OKLAHOMA

ACF of Central Oklahoma
Mrs. Genni Thomas
4337 Dahoon Drive
Oklahoma City, OK 73120
Work (405) 755-1515
Home (405) 752-1279

OREGON

Chefs de Cuisine Society of Oregon
David Angell, CCE
c/o Western Culinary Institute
1316 S.W. 13th Avenue
Portland, OR 97201
Work (503) 223-2245
Home (503) 224-2532

ACF Southern Oregon Chapter
Russell Rickert
164 Almeda
Ashland, OR 97520
Work (503) 826-1303
Home (503) 482-8704

PENNSYLVANIA

ACF Laurel Highlands Chapter
Marlene Scatena, R.D.
Westmoreland County Community College
Culinary Arts
Armbrust Road
Youngwood, PA 15697-1895
Work (412) 925-4000

Central Pennsylvania Chefs Association
Walter Schaffhauser, CEC, AAC
1020 Orange Street
Steelton, PA 17113
Work (717) 939-2858

Delaware Valley Chefs Association
Walter Grund
7980 Oxford
Philadelphia, PA 19111
Work (215) 728-1065

ACF, Professional Chefs of Northeast Pennsylvania
George R. Cron, CWC
715 Cedar Avenue
Scranton, PA 18505
Work (717) 969-0639

Chefs Association of Pittsburgh
Willie Stinson, CEC
Culinary Arts Program
Community College of Allegheny County
808 Ridge Avenue
Pittsburgh, PA 15212
Work (412) 237-2598

Pocono Professional Chefs Association
Howard Newhard, Jr., CEC
Rd. 6, Box 6124
Stroudsburg, PA 18360

Work (717) 992-4969
Home (717) 992-6855

RHODE ISLAND

ACF Rhode Island Chapter
  Theodore A. Butzbach, CEC, CCE
  14 D Caddy Rock Road
  North Kingston, RI 02815
  Work (401) 828-7800 Ext. 264
  Home (401) 294-4174

Newport, Rhode Island Chapter of the ACF
  Roger S. Valentine, Executive Chef
  Newport Marriott Hotel
  25 America's Cup Avenue
  Newport, RI 02840
  Work (401) 849-1000

SOUTH CAROLINA

Hilton Head Island Chefs Association
  Robert Hartner
  Post Office Box 1766
  Hilton Head Island, SC 29925
  Work (803) 681-4000 Ext. 7370
  Home (803) 681-3782

ACF Charleston Chapter
  Kim Kearse
  Route 5, Box 2
  Moncks Corner, SC 29461
  Work (803) 722-5571

TENNESSEE

ACF Middle Tennessee Chapter
  Eric Dincewze
  923 Downey Drive
  Nashville, TN 37205
  Work (615) 356-0035
  Home (615) 373-3200

Opryland Hotel
  Richard Gerst
  2800 Opryland Drive
  Nashville, TN 37214
  Work (615) 889-1000

ACF Greater Memphis Chapter
  Steve Scranton
  c/o Baptist Memorial Hospital
  899 Madison Avenue
  Memphis, TN 38146
  Work (901) 522-5054

TEXAS

Texas Chefs Association—Austin
  Levell "Bud" Wheeler
  1905 Egger Avenue
  Round Rock, TX 78664
  Work (512) 244-0534

Texas Chefs Association—Dallas
  James Goering, CCE, CES
  El Centro College
  Main at Lamar
  Dallas, TX 78734
  Work (214) 746-2217
  Home (214) 241-4487

Texas Chefs Association—Houston
  Hans Huwyler
  6706 Spring Cypress Road
  Spring, TX 77379
  Work (713) 458-4050

Texas Chefs Association—San Antonio
  Bill Phipps, CEC
  9839 Spruce Ridge
  Converse, TX 78109
  Work (512) 822-8722

UTAH

ACF Beehive State Chefs Chapter
  Gary Pankow/Apprenticeship
  Salt Lake City Community College
  4600 South Redwood Road
  Salt Lake City, UT 84130
  Work (801) 967-4066
  Home (801) 350-5697

VERMONT

North Vermont Chefs & Cooks Association
  Kevin dRaper
  R.D. 1, Box 2620
  Waterbury Center, VT 05677
  Work (802) 434-2131 Ext. 354
  Home (802) 244-5851

Appendix B

VIRGINIA

Virginia Chefs Association
  Mark Kimmel, CEC
  7212 Bennington Road
  Richmond, VA 23225
  Work (804) 782-9432
  Home (804) 745-1647

Pierre Monet, CEC
  The Colonial Williamsburg
  Foundation
  Post Office Box Drawer B
  Williamsburg, VA 23187
  Work (804) 229-1000 Ext. 4306

Blue Ridge Chefs Association
  W. B. King, Executive Chef
  University of Virginia
  Post Office Box 9020
  Charlottesville, VA 22906
  Work (804) 924-7781
  Home (804) 973-8634

WASHINGTON

Washington State Chefs Association
  David Estes
  30218 Second Avenue South
  Federal Way, WA 98003
  Work (206) 433-2524
  Home (206) 946-4466

WISCONSIN

Professional Chefs and Cooks of Milwaukee
  Knut Apitz
  Grenadier's Restaurant
  747 North Broadway at Mason
  Milwaukee, WI 53202
  Work (414) 276-0747

ACF Fox Valley Chapter
  Albert Exenberger
  Fox Valley Technical Institute
  1825 North Bluemound Drive
  Post Office Box 2277
  Appleton, WI 54913-2277
  Work (414) 735-5600

ACCREDITING COMMISSION—ACCREDITATION ACTIVITY

CALIFORNIA

ORANGE COAST COLLEGE
  2710 Fairview Blvd.
  Costa Mesa, CA 92625
  STATUS: Accredited to 6/30/90
  PROGRAMS: Certificates in Advanced Culinary Arts and Cook Apprentice, A. A. Degree in Culinary Arts

FLORIDA

FLORIDA VO-TECH INSTITUTE
  6100 154th Avenue
  North Clearwater, FL 33516
  STATUS: Accredited to 6/30/90
  PROGRAM: Diploma in Culinary Arts

ST. AUGUSTINE TECHNICAL CENTER
  Collins at Del Monte Avenue
  St. Augustine, FL 32084
  STATUS: Accredited to 12/31/92
  PROGRAM: Diploma in Culinary Arts

ILLINOIS

ELGIN COMMUNITY COLLEGE
  Culinary Arts Department
  1700 Spartan Drive
  Elgin, IL 60120
  STATUS: Accredited to 12/31/92
  PROGRAMS: A.A.S. Degree in Culinary Arts and Hospitality Management

JOLIET JUNIOR COLLEGE
  1216 Hubolt Avenue
  Joliet, IL 60436

PROGRAMS: A.A.S. Degree in Culinary Arts

KENDALL COLLEGE
2408 Orrington Avenue
Evanston, IL 60201
STATUS: Accredited to 6/30/91
PROGRAM: A.A.S. Degree in Culinary Arts

INDIANA

INDIANA VO-TECH COLLEGE
Post Office Box 1763
Indianapolis, IN 46206
STATUS: Accredited to 12/31/92
PROGRAM: A.A.S. Degree in Culinary Arts

KANSAS

JOHNSON COUNTY COMMUNITY COLLEGE
12345 College at Quivira
Overland Park, KS 66210
STATUS: Accredited to 12/31/91
PROGRAM: A.A.S. Degree in Hospitality Management and Chef Apprenticeship

KENTUCKY

JEFFERSON COMMUNITY COLLEGE
109 East Broadway
Louisville, KY 40202
STATUS: Accredited to 6/30/92
PROGRAM: A.A.S. Degree in Culinary Arts

MARYLAND

BALTIMORE'S INTERNATIONAL CULINARY
COLLEGE
19-21 South Gay Street
Baltimore, MD 21202
STATUS: Accredited to 12/31/91
PROGRAMS: A.A. Degrees in Restaurant & Cooking Skills and Baking & Pastry

MICHIGAN

GRAND RAPIDS JUNIOR
143 Bostwick, N.E.
Grand Rapids, MI 49503
STATUS: Accredited to 12/31/92
PROGRAMS: Degrees in Culinary Arts and Food & Beverage Management

NORTHWESTERN MICHIGAN COLLEGE
1701 East Front Street
Traverse City, MI 49684
STATUS: Accredited to 12/31/92
PROGRAM: A.A.S. Degree in Food Service Management

MINNESOTA

HENNEPIN TECHNICAL CENTERS
9000 Brooklyn Boulevard
Brooklyn Park, MN 55445
STATUS: Accredited to 12/31/92
PROGRAM: Diploma in Cook/Chef

NORTHEAST METRO TECHNICAL INSTITUTE
3300 Century Avenue, North
White Bear Lake, MN 55110
STATUS: Accredited to 6/30/93
PROGRAM: Diploma in Chef Training

MONTANA

MISSOULA VO-TECH CENTER
90 South Avenue West
Missoula, MT 59801
STATUS: Accredited to 6/30/93
PROGRAM: Certificate in Kitchen Production Management

NEW YORK

SULLIVAN COUNTY COMMUNITY COLLEGE
Hospitality Department
Loch Sheldrake, NY 12759
STATUS: Accredited to 12/31/92

PROGRAMS: A.A.S. Degrees in Food Service
Administration and Restaurant Management; Certificate in Food Service

SUNY/COBLESKILL AGRICULTURE AND TECHNICAL COLLEGE
Cobleskill, NY 12043
STATUS: Accredited to 12/31/92
PROGRAM: A.O.S. Degree—Professional Chef

OHIO

CINCINNATI TECHNICAL COLLEGE
3520 Central Parkway
Cincinnati, OH 45223
STATUS: Accredited to 12/31/91
PROGRAM: Associate Degree in Applied Business in Chef Technology

COLUMBUS STATE COMMUNITY COLLEGE
550 East Spring Street
Columbus, OH 43215
STATUS: Accredited to 12/31/91
PROGRAMS: A.A.S. Degrees in Food Service, Restaurant Management, and Chef Apprenticeship

OREGON

WESTERN CULINARY INSTITUTE
316 S.W. 13th Avenue
Portland, OR 97201
STATUS: Accredited to 6/30/93
PROGRAM: Diploma in Culinary Arts

PENNSYLVANIA

WESTMORELAND COUNTY COMMUNITY COLLEGE
Armhurst Road
Youngwood, PA 15697
STATUS: Accredited to 12/31/92
PROGRAMS: A.A.S. Degrees in Food Service Management and Culinary Arts

SOUTH CAROLINA

GREENVILLE TECHNICAL COLLEGE
Post Office Box 5616, Station B
Greenville, SC 19606
STATUS: Accredited to 12/31/93
PROGRAM: A.B. Degree in Food Service Management

WASHINGTON

SOUTH SEATTLE COMMUNITY COLLEGE
6000 16th Avenue, S.W.
Seattle, WA 98106
STATUS: Accredited to 12/31/93
PROGRAMS: A.A.S. Degree in Hospitality and Food Service; Certificate in Food Science Production Management

WISCONSIN

MILWAUKEE AREA TECHNICAL COLLEGE
1015 North Sixth Street
Milwaukee, WI 53203
STATUS: Accredited to 6/30/92
PROGRAM: A.A.S. Degree in Restaurant & Hotel Cookery and Apprentice Cook